The junior church programme with a difference!

Three + One

Great kings

Michael Forster

Kevin Mayhew

Margot

First published in 2000 by
KEVIN MAYHEW LTD
Buxhall
Stowmarket
Suffolk IP14 3BW

0 1 2 3 4 5 6 7 8 9

ISBN 1 84003 583 8
Catalogue No 1500368

Cover illustration by Jonathan Stroulger
Illustrated by Simon Smith
Edited by Helen Elliot
Typesetting by Elisabeth Bates
Printed in Great Britain

Contents

Foreword

This series of books takes what might to many people seem to be a new approach to Junior Church teaching and all-age worship. In fact, though, it's a very old one – used, according to the Gospels, by Jesus himself.

First and foremost, Jesus valued people, cared about them, was concerned for their needs. He called people to become part of a community where they – many of them for the first time – were valued and enabled to feel that they were part of something worthwhile, that their lives had meaning and purpose. In the course of that, they learned a great deal and their commitment to Jesus and what he stood for grew until in many cases it was a life-commitment in more ways than one.

So the approach we take here is to focus on building relationships – including the children in something they may come to value, telling the faith story in engaging ways and letting the 'learning' be a spin-off benefit. I am convinced that that is a more effective way of working with children than focusing just on the imparting of knowledge.

People often complain that youth organisations do not seem 'interested in the Church'. The reality is that there is no *reason* for them to be interested: without faith commitment there is no other point in going to church when everything else it offers can be had more easily and more satisfyingly elsewhere. And that faith commitment will, I believe, be built more effectively, in their early years, by making them part of something they value *because it values them* rather than by trying to teach them things.

That brings me to the vital difference that sets this material apart. The sessions are arranged in sets of four: three 'Junior Church' sessions building into an all-age service on the fourth Sunday when the children's work will be celebrated and valued by the whole Church fellowship, and the adults will have the opportunity to learn both from and with the children.

I hope and pray that these resources will open minds of all ages to the wonder of God's love and the joy of sharing it, rather than merely fill them up with doctrines and ethical propositions.

All that will follow. The first thing – and the vital thing – is to *relate.*

Enjoy the book. Enjoy one another. Oh, and enjoy God, of course!

MICHAEL FORSTER

Introduction

(Please read this – I think you're going to like it!)

This series of books arose out of a particular need. We were finding the usual age-based 'classes' difficult to sustain in our context, and mixed-age groups seemed the only option – but the cry went up, 'You can't teach five- and ten-year-olds in the same class' (I'll have more to say about the 'teaching' idea later).

At the same time, we wanted to include the children much more in the actual planning of our monthly all-age worship which, until then, tended to be a bit of a one-man show that was done *for* rather than *with* them. But just when do you gather increasingly busy and pressurised children together to plan services?

This is what we decided to do. We would take an overall theme that could be presented in three weekly stories, and the learning process would consist of fun activities: story-telling, art and craft, drama, music, some of which could then become the basis for the all-age service. But what if some children could only come for two of the weeks? Would they be left out? Clearly, each week's story, while relating to the three-week theme, would need to be able to stand alone.

Wouldn't it make the all-age worship terribly long and overladen with material? Probably, if *all* the previous three-weeks' work were used – so the Junior Church would choose just one of the three stories as the focus for the service, but let the worship leader put it into context with the help of the pictures, models, etc., that the children had made. That would enable most of the art and craftwork to be on display in the church, providing a visual background to the storytelling. And storytelling really is the basis of communicating our faith. Ask any of our Jewish cousins! Or ask Jesus!

So this material was written, and some of it has been used, and the basic idea and format have been tried and tested. The result so far has been the releasing of some previously unrecognised creativity as children who had not been in the limelight before took the basic ideas and developed them in wonderfully imaginative ways. In the very first month of using this material, we discovered some real hidden treasure – and we did so in worship where we could properly celebrate and give thanks for it.

And that brings me to the most important thing we learned from this. Don't let the all-age worship become a talking shop! The discussion-type activities will quickly lose their appeal if that happens. We saw this coming in good time and proposed the setting up of a Worship and Mission Action Group (definitely *not* a committee) within the church to carry forward some of the ideas that come out of these sessions. Such a group must be a 'ginger group' rather than a management committee. They should not get bogged down in the minutiae of keeping new projects going, but simply research ideas and present possibilities to the relevant meetings (more than once if necessary!) to ensure that they are not simply lost in a sea of good intentions. If that were to happen – if the cards, etc., that the discussion groups produce were simply thrown away or filed and forgotten, we think it would not be long before the worship became stale: 'Oh, another of those silly discussions, again.' However, if the action group is set up, and enabled to work well, the all-age worship could become a real source of inspiration for the Church's mission – something through which the Holy Spirit might breathe renewal into the Church and the local community.

How to get the best from this book

The book is based on three 'units', each of which is a four-week cycle: three Junior Church sessions, and one all-age worship. Those Churches that currently have a monthly 'family service' will find it best to plan so that the 'fourth' Sunday in each unit falls on whatever Sunday of the month is appropriate for their system. (When there are five Sundays, that's not a problem – you'll appreciate the extra time to pull the threads together all the more firmly ready for the all-age service.)

Each session divides into a number of activities, and a worksheet is also provided either to do in the session or as a take-home resource. There will almost certainly be too much here for the single session of perhaps 45 minutes that most Junior Churches have – so *don't think you have to use it all.* (Nothing destroys a good learning environment like trying to cram too much in!) Choose what you think best fits your group in each particular case, and perhaps have other items standing by in case you run out. Much of course will depend on the number of children you have. A small Junior Church could work all together, concentrating on the story and just one or two activities, whereas a large one might start together for the storytelling and then break up into several multi-age groups, each focusing on a different activity – some children producing art and craft work, others doing drama, learning new songs, etc.

Similarly, you don't need necessarily to use all of sessions one to three. You may decide, in particular circumstances, to omit one session and spread the other two over the three weeks. The stories are written as stand-alone units, so you can do this quite easily. At the risk of labouring the point, the all-age worship in Week Four should be a celebration of whatever has been done – not a goal to be striven for and which becomes a blight on the sessions because the children are under pressure.

Most importantly of all, remember the central aims: the session should:

- be enjoyable for all concerned
- make all the children feel valued and cared about
- contribute to building relationships.

If you do these things, then the 'teaching' will happen, because children are great learners if the environment is right. They'll virtually teach themselves!

Let's have a look at each of the elements that comprise the sessions.

Thinking about it

This is vital – the advance preparation need not be unduly time-consuming or tedious, but it will transform the actual session. In fact, we found that the preparation required in using this material was much less onerous than preparing traditional lessons.

- A monthly meeting of key people would be a good idea, perhaps after Week Three, when you can pull together the all-age service and look ahead to the next four weeks.

- Decide which week's subtheme will form the basis of the all-age worship. You need to know this at the outset so that you will know which week's 'ticked' activity to prepare and which you can ignore.
- Then each week look through the relevant session thoroughly and give some thought to which would be the most appropriate and helpful elements to concentrate on, in your situation.
- Prepare any resources: art/craft materials, visual aids, legitimate photocopies, etc., that you need. Try to anticipate the kinds of questions the children might ask – or that you could helpfully ask them.

What's the point?

It's helpful to have a specific point in mind that we wish to convey. This does not mean we can't find other things in the text, but one point retained is better than five confused or forgotten – and more likely to engage the children's attention, too! They have the rest of their lives to explore the countless layers of meaning, so don't let's spoil it by cramming them too full of rich food!

Now for the session itself.

Doing it

Prayer

An opening prayer is offered. However, we should be careful about stereotyping prayer too much as merely 'talking to God'. It might be worth thinking about encouraging children to think of prayer as consciously *being with* God – sometimes quietly, but also in the more active parts of life. So let God join in the activities, the fun, most of all in the growing *relationships* between staff, parents and children. In a different kind of way, the whole session is 'prayer' – and both kinds are important.

For this reason, the prayers are short and are all focused in such a way as to point the children to that greater reality: the unconditional love of God.

From the known to the unknown

Jesus understood well the first principle of teaching: begin with what people know, and only then introduce the new. His most effective teaching, according to the Gospel records, was in parables. Often, he simply didn't mention scripture at all.

That is not an argument against biblical teaching – rather it is a plea to make it more effective. Children are wonderful at making connections – much better than we adults with our 'disciplined' (trammeled?) minds. So we begin by appealing to what they know, and *then* tell them the biblical story. With little or no prompting, they often will then grasp joyfully and spontaneously for themselves what we so often labour painfully and ineffectually to drill into them – and no one's more guilty of that than I am!

Tell the story

Story-telling is the basis of keeping the faith alive. Our Jewish forebears kept their children in the faith by telling and retelling vibrant stories, often around meal-tables, camp fires or in other informal settings, with plenty of song and laughter to help it along. So a child-friendly version of a Bible story is the mainstay of each week's material. It's a good idea to read it a few times in advance, so you are familiar and can half-tell, half-read it to the children with plenty of eye contact and other interaction. Or you can get them to tell it to each other by acting it out – see 'Drama', below. You may also find it useful to have some visual aids handy, or think of some questions you can ask, breaking off from the narrative whenever you choose to ask, 'How do you think God felt about that?' 'What d'you think happened then?' 'What would you have done about that?' etc. This will all help to maintain the children's interest – with a little imagination you can easily keep them enthralled!

Respond to the story

The children's response to the story now forms the basis of the rest of the session. It's important that they're encouraged to be spontaneous and really engage with the characters and the action. Here you will of course want to focus on the forms of response that are best suited to your situation, but the first one, 'Discussion', should never be missed out.

Discussion

Keep it lively, informal, chatty – and don't let any child feel silly or wrong, whatever they say or ask. The important thing is that they grow by being able to interact freely with the text. You may want to feed in some of their questions or reactions to the storytelling in the all-age worship. Most importantly, don't be anxious about this section – and don't let the discussion become either too long or too heavy! Just enjoy a bit of a chat with the children.

Song

Some songs are suggested. Either revisiting well-known ones or learning new ones can be fun, and perhaps sometimes the children can teach some of the new ones to the adults in the all-age worship. However, be careful not to let the Junior Church session degenerate into mere rehearsal. Let them have fun singing the songs, confident that even imperfectly sung they will still form acceptable worship. If some of the children have instruments, there's no reason why they couldn't be used at this time. All the songs recommended in these pages can be found in one or more of the following Kevin Mayhew publications (among others):

- *Kidsource*
- *The Source*
- *The Children's Hymn Book*
- *21st Century Folk Hymnal*

Art and craft

This will probably form quite a big part of the session: children of all ages and abilities can work together to produce models, drawings, paintings, etc. A few ideas are suggested, but they don't need to be limited. This was the area where we found children really showed their ingenuity and made immensely valuable contributions, producing and effecting ideas that would never have occurred to us!

Some of the art and craft work will feed into the all-age worship, and the items especially designed to do that are indicated with a tick. You may want to put less emphasis on this item if you're not planning on focusing on it in the service. What is important, in the 'ticked' activities, is that the children know *why* they are preparing these things – a few simple words of explanation will help them to relate it to the story they have heard and the point you were trying to make.

In terms of drawing and painting, the options are limited only by size of the group and the children's imaginations! They could build up over the three weeks a complete 'strip cartoon' of the whole story, to be used in introducing the theme in all-age worship. The pictures could be on a continuous frieze, or on cardboard placards held on poles by the children, or separate pictures fixed around the walls before the service starts. Children could enter at different points as the story is told, holding their placard, or – well, you think of your own ideas – they'll probably be better than mine, anyway.

Drama

The dramatised version of the story is included. It can simply be used as a dramatised reading, with different children literally reading the parts, or it could be developed if your group has a flair for it into something much bigger. Adapt it freely to suit your group. If you need more parts, try splitting the narrator's part between several children, or add in one or two new characters. During the free discussion of the story things might emerge that it would be good to include in the dialogue. Feel free to photocopy these pages and make your own alterations if you wish. The drama can then either be used simply as a teaching aid or rehearsed and presented in the all-age worship. An added touch might be to use a domestic tape recorder to record it – then each child could take home a recording of a play with their own voice on it!

Worksheet

This is included for you to use as you see fit. You could have some of the children colour in the pictures and display them at the service, or you could let a group work through the sheet as part of the session; or it could simply be given to them as a take-home sheet to help them remember the session and/or to share with their families.

All-age worship

This is the culmination of the unit, but please don't allow preparation for it to dominate and spoil the sessions. It's not a performance, and no one will mind if what the children produce isn't beautifully polished – the main thing is that they should be seen to be enjoying it.

The services are designed to be truly 'all age', involving the whole congregation, and – most importantly – giving opportunities for interaction across the age groups. There are no 'children's talks', but rather all-age activities. This approach needs to be reflected in the overall balance of the service, so that it is one in which all people can participate rather than a children's service with the adults as indulgent spectators.

Let's take a look at the various elements:

Songs

Naturally, there will be songs specifically chosen by the children, or at least with them in mind. But including some more 'adult' hymns not only shows respect to the older worshippers but also requires the children to sample a more varied diet and hopefully broaden their taste.

Welcome and statement of the theme

An example is given, but please feel free to use your own words and adapt it for your own circumstances. It's an important element in the service, for it introduces the chosen theme and sets it in the wider context. It is also a jolly good opportunity to point out some of the creative work the children have done, and have it suitably acknowledged by the congregation.

Prayers

Again, an opening prayer is offered, but it's not mandatory! Local worship leaders will probably want to do something more appropriate to the particular setting.

Word and action

The Bible story selected from one of the weeks 1-3 is not only read but reinforced with an all-age activity. The essential point is to make this at once meaningful and enjoyable. If people enjoy it, they're far more likely to enter into it. One important point, though: you know your own congregation best, and are in a position to ensure that people aren't treated insensitively. If you know that Mrs X doesn't like being in the limelight, then avoid drawing attention to her. Finally, watch the time. People will warm to the subject and be difficult to stop! You will also then be deluged with responses, many of them duplicated in different groups. Keep the discussion short and to the point, and move on. And don't forget to consider setting up the action group (see Introduction, page 7) – people need to know this isn't just a talking shop!

Offertory prayer

All we do and give is a free response to what God does for and gives to us. The offertory prayer is a good opportunity to highlight that point. This helps to avoid religion becoming 'works centred' rather than being a free, joyful response to God's grace.

Reading

Because you're using imaginatively rewritten stories, it's very important to read from a standard Bible in the service, and this point should never be overlooked. Children – and especially the older ones and the young people – need to hear the Bible read and come to appreciate it for themselves.

Talk

It's marked 'optional', but it's actually quite an important part of the service. As with the Bible, the traditional sermon is too valuable (when done well) to throw away. In a service of this nature, a short talk helps develop and maintain the skills of listening and reasoning. Keep it short, though, or it will have the opposite effect! On the other hand, if the service is running over time, this is an element that could *occasionally* be omitted.

Notices and family news

All too often, notices are regarded as an intrusion, and ways are often found to 'get them out of the way'. But surely, this is the life of the Church that is being shared here – and should it not be offered to God, along with the lives of his people? In the service order, I've suggested putting the notices directly before the Intercessions, so they can then feed into the prayers, thus integrating them more closely into the worship.

This is also a suitable time to do something else – the 'Family News'. People who have, for example, a birthday, or a wedding anniversary, or perhaps who are changing jobs, retiring or whatever, can share that with the congregation. A supply of cards can be kept in the church, with a suitably general message in them, to be handed out to people along with the good wishes and applause of the congregation. This is one slot we daren't leave out at Anstey, or we hear about it!

Intercessions

If Jesus was 'the man for others', it's hard to imagine worship that is genuinely Christian and doesn't include some sort of intercession for others. You will certainly want to include some of the children's own concerns that have emerged in the sessions in these prayers. You might also want to use some of the artwork to help the congregation focus on particular things. Whoever leads these, try to ensure that they are done thoughtfully, with a concern for the whole of God's creation, and not just Christians.

Closing prayer/benediction

Another element that should be kept short but meaningful! This is where the congregation are sent out into the world to live in some way the values and ideals they have expressed in their worship.

Now, go to it!

Most importantly of all – use the material imaginatively; make it work *for you*. It is your servant, not your director. What matters is that all involved enjoy the sessions, learn about valuing and being valued, build relationships with each other and with 'staff', and learn along the way.

That's how Jesus worked whenever he could. And it's not a bad example to follow!

Unit 1
David – little but large

Overview of the unit

We take three key events:

Week 1: Samuel anoints David

Outward appearances can be deceptive – and God's way of judging people goes a lot deeper than ours.

Week 2: David and Goliath

Goliath was a bully and, when challenged, turned out to have little there to back up the bluster. Sometimes we all have to stand up to 'Goliaths', whether individual, political, commercial, etc. – and it's good to know that it can be done in the name of God.

Week 3: David and Bathsheba

Had King David known, when he first looked over the balcony and saw Bathsheba, what a catastrophic series of unpredictable consequences he would unleash, it's possible he might have decided to nip the whole episode in the bud there and then. However, as he didn't, we can not only learn a salutary lesson from his experience but find reassurance from the fact that even such a fall from grace did not prevent God from making him a great king.

All-age worship

Here, you may choose to focus on any one of the three subthemes, but place it in the context of the overall story and theme. So while the specific subtheme chosen will be emphasised in the choice of 'Word and action' material, some of the art and craft work the children have done in the other weeks will be used to decorate the church and set the context of the wider story.

Important note

✔ The ticked activities in Weeks 1-3 are intended as the link material for the 'Word and action' slot in the all-age worship. You will only need to do this in one of the three weeks – depending on which week's subtheme is going to be the main emphasis in the service.

Week 1: Samuel anoints David

Thinking about it

What's the point?

Often we judge by outward appearances, but God 'looks at the heart' – and we might be a lot fairer to people if we followed his example!

Doing it

Prayer

Loving God,
thank you for knowing us so well.
Be with us in this time we share together,
and help us to get to know each other better.
Amen.

From the known to the unknown

Have some 'presents' wrapped up in advance – some very impressive packages with either nothing or something trivial inside, and some less well-presented ones containing things of greater value. To emphasise the point, you might put a very valuable item (such as a ring) into a scruffy paper bag. (A ring's a good idea because you can put it safely on your finger after you've unwrapped it!)

To avoid disappointments, tell the children before you show them the parcels that you're going to unwrap *your* presents in front of them. Start with the most glamorous packages and work your way 'down' to the paper bag. The moral's not difficult to see!

Tell the story: 1 Samuel 16:1-13

(See page 21 for a dramatised version of this story)

A Funny Sort of King

Samuel the prophet was having a bad day. 'But God,' he protested, 'it was you who told me to anoint Saul as king of Israel in the first place – and now you want me to anoint another?'

'Not much to ask,' God answered. 'Just a matter of pouring a bit of oil over someone's head and saying that I've chosen him to be king – now what's so difficult about that?'

'Oh, just one little detail,' Samuel replied. 'Like, Saul's still alive, and he thought he was king for life, and I don't think he's going to take this lying down. Like, he'll kill me?'

'Come on, Sam, tell it how it is,' said God, sternly. 'You've been moaning about what a rotten king Saul is for years, and I agree he's got it all wrong

– big time – so now you've got the chance to do something about it. Go to Bethlehem and pay a visit to Jesse the sheep farmer. Tell him you've come to hold a special service, or something – just do it.'

When Samuel arrived, Jesse was worried because he knew Samuel was a powerful man in Israel. 'What have I done now?' he asked.

'Nothing,' returned Samuel, 'I'm here on a peaceful mission.'

'Then you're very welcome,' said Jesse. 'I was only just saying there's no profit in sheep farming and here you are. "Profit", "prophet" – get it? Oh, please yourself.'

Samuel groaned. Why did he always get the smart Alecs to deal with? 'I've come to hold a special service,' he said, 'so go and get washed and let's just get on with it.'

Jesse went and called his sons. Eliab was the first to arrive. 'Ah, now there's a fine looking young man,' Samuel thought. 'A quick drop of oil in that nice wavy hair and I can be gone while he's trying to wash it out.'

'Not so fast,' said God. 'I haven't chosen him. You're just looking at the outside – I look at what's inside.'

'You must have a stronger stomach than mine,' thought Samuel. 'OK, let's see the next one.'

'Here's Abinadab,' said Jesse. 'Good strong lad, don't you think?'

'That's true,' thought Samuel. 'Looks like a man who can take care of himself – and a purple robe would go well with that bruise on his cheekbone.'

'Not this one, either,' God whispered to Samuel. 'Have a look at another one.'

'You make it sound like buying a used chariot,' Samuel thought.

'I wouldn't know,' God answered. 'I'm glad to say I have never had to make do with a *used* chariot.'

'Oh, very funny,' Samuel sighed to himself. 'Now I've got God being clever, as well as Jesse.'

'I heard that,' said God. 'Keep your mind on your work. Here's another son coming. It's Shammah, and before you get any ideas, he's not the one, either.'

'Sorry, Jesse,' said Samuel, 'Have you got any more?'

'Oh, I think I could rustle up a few more,' Jesse replied with a grin. '"Rustle", sheep farming? Get it? No, I thought not.'

Jesse showed seven sons to Samuel, and Samuel just kept saying, 'No, this isn't the one.' Even Jesse's humour was beginning to wear thin.

'Are you going to tell me what's going on?' he demanded. 'These are my sons you're looking at – this isn't a cattle market, you know.'

'No,' said Samuel, dryly, 'it's a sheep farm – so just you keep them coming.'

'Oh, very smart,' answered Jesse. 'Well, there's only one left – my youngest, David – he's out in the fields looking after the sheep.'

When David arrived, Samuel began to despair. This was no king in waiting: small, lightweight, and very, very young – hardly the kind of impressive figure to lead strong men into battle.

'That's the one! That's the one! Wonderful! Just the one for the job.' God seemed to be getting quite unnecessarily excited. 'Go on, Sam – give him the works!'

So the day ended, with Samuel very tired, David washing his hair and Jesse wondering what on earth it had all been about. But Samuel couldn't help being hopeful about the future. David didn't seem very impressive compared with King Saul, but there was something about him.

It had been a long day, and Samuel was no sooner home than he was sound asleep. And talking of sounds, could he be dreaming, or was that God laughing?

Respond to the story

Discussion

What does this story tell us about God?

- That he cares about what kind of people we are, not what we look like?
- That he can do wonderful things with us however unpromising we seem?

What sort of things would the children do if they were king or queen?

- Abolish maths lessons?
- Build homes for all the homeless people?
- Provide more play areas for children?

What sort of things might a *bad* king or queen do?

- Take other children's toys for themselves?
- Turn the children's playground into a private castle?
- Have everyone they don't like locked up?
- What else?

Song

One or more of the following songs might be used here and/or in the all-age worship:

I'm gonna click, click, click
Lovely in your littleness
Nobody's a nobody
When the Spirit of the Lord is within my heart

Art and craft

✔ Make simple cardboard crowns to fit three of the children, paint them gold and put a large number 1, 2 or 3 on the front. (See 'Word and action' in the all-age worship for how this would be used.) Then fold three A4 cards in half like greetings cards. Using the ideas raised in the discussion, write each king or queen a manifesto on the front of their card, saying what good things they will do if they are chosen. Then, inside one of the cards, write a lot of bad things under a heading such as 'What I would *really* do'. Inside the other cards write 'This is true'. Make sure there are no clues as to which card is the bad one – and don't decide at this point which of the three children is going to hold it – they probably won't be able to keep the secret for the next three weeks! You may find it helpful to make a number of photocopies of the fronts of the cards to give out at the all-age worship as *aides memoires* for the congregation, but do *not* include the insides.

Draw or paint a picture of Samuel anointing David.

This is the key picture, but you might want to do others in addition to it, such as:

- Samuel looking at one or more of David's (impressive) brothers
- David in the field caring for the sheep.

Drama

See the next page for a dramatised version of the story

Drama: A Funny Sort of King

Narrator Samuel the prophet was having a bad day.

Samuel But God, it was you who told me to anoint Saul as king of Israel in the first place – and now you want me to anoint another?

God Just a matter of pouring a bit of oil over someone's head and saying that he's my chosen king – now what's so hard about that?

Samuel Oh, just one little detail – like, Saul's still alive, and I don't think he's going to take this lying down. Like, he'll kill me?

God Come on, Sam – you've been moaning about what a rotten king Saul is for years, and I agree. So now you've got the chance to do something about it. Go to Bethlehem and pay a visit to Jesse the sheep farmer. Tell him you've come to hold a special service, or something – just do it.

Narrator When Samuel arrived, Jesse was worried because he knew Samuel was a powerful man in Israel.

Jesse What have I done now?

Samuel Nothing, I'm here on a peaceful mission.

Jesse Then you're very welcome. I was only just saying there's no profit in sheep farming and here you are. 'Profit', 'prophet' – get it? Oh, please yourself.

Samuel [*Aside*] Oh, why do I always get the smart Alecs to deal with? [*To Jesse*] I've come to hold a special service, so go and get washed and let's just get on with it.

Narrator Jesse went and called his sons. Eliab was the first to arrive.

Samuel [*Aside*] What a fine looking young man. A quick drop of oil in that nice wavy hair and I can be gone while he's trying to wash it out.

God Not so fast. I haven't chosen him. You're just looking at the outside – I look at what's inside.

Samuel You must have a stronger stomach than mine. OK, Jesse, let's see the next one.

Jesse Here's Abinadab. Good strong lad, don't you think?

Samuel That's true – looks like a man who can take care of himself – and a purple robe would go well with that bruise on his cheek-bone.

God Not this one, either, Sam. Have a look at another one.

Samuel You make it sound like buying a used chariot.

God I wouldn't know – I'm glad to say I have never had to make do with a *used* chariot.

Samuel [*Aside*] Oh, very funny! Now I've got God being clever, as well as Jesse.

God I heard that. Keep your mind on your work. Here's another son coming. It's Shammah, and before you get any ideas, he's not the one, either.

Samuel Sorry, Jesse. Have you got any more?

Jesse [*Grinning*] Oh, I think I could *rustle up* a few more. 'Rustle' – sheep farming? Get it? [*Samuel looks blank*] No, I thought not.

Narrator Jesse showed seven sons to Samuel, and Samuel just kept saying 'No'. Even Jesse's humour was beginning to wear thin.

Jesse Are you going to tell me what's going on? These are my sons you're looking at – this isn't a cattle market, you know.

Samuel No, it's a sheep farm – so just you keep them coming.

Jesse Oh, very smart. Well, there's only one left – my youngest, David – he's out in the fields looking after the sheep.

Narrator When David arrived, Samuel began to despair. This was no king in waiting: small, lightweight, and very, very young – hardly the kind of impressive figure to lead strong men into battle.

God [*Excitedly*] That's the one! That's the one! Wonderful! Just the one for the job. Go on, Sam – give him the works!

Narrator So the day ended, with Samuel very tired, David washing his hair and Jesse wondering what on earth it had all been about. But Samuel couldn't help being hopeful about the future. David didn't seem very impressive compared with King Saul, but there was something about him. It had been a long day, and Samuel was no sooner home than he was sound asleep. And talking of sounds, could he be dreaming, or was that God laughing?

God looks at the heart. (1 Samuel 16:7)

WORDSEARCH

Find the following words in the grid:
SAMUEL, SAUL, BETHLEHEM, KING, ABINADAB, ANOINT, DAVID, JESSE, GOD, SHAMMAH, OIL, SHEEP.

S	A	M	U	E	T	L	E	U	M	A	S
H	N	O	I	N	T	B	E	T	H	L	A
E	O	A	K	I	N	J	J	E	S	S	U
E	I	B	E	T	H	L	E	H	E	M	L
D	A	I	V	D	M	A	H	S	A	U	T
B	A	N	O	I	N	T	H	E	S	A	E
E	B	A	H	V	A	B	I	H	A	E	S
T	I	D	L	A	B	F	A	S	M	D	S
H	N	A	I	D	I	M	H	D	U	A	G
L	A	B	O	N	M	G	O	C	E	V	N
E	D	G	S	A	A	A	B	I	G	I	I
H	E	E	H	X	D	S	H	E	E	P	K

Find which box contains the treasure.

TRUE OR FALSE?

David was the biggest of his brothers.
God judges us by how we look.
God can make ordinary people great.
Samuel was a sheep farmer.
God is more trustworthy than we often realise.

Week 2: David and Goliath

Thinking about it

What's the point?

The world is full of apparently powerless people who are oppressed by bullies of one kind or another – whether individuals, governments, big business or whatever. It's important to know that it's worth standing up to these Goliaths.

Doing it

Prayer

Loving God,
thank you for caring about us all,
whether we seem important to others or not.
Help us to enjoy today's session,
to have fun together,
and also to grow more confident that you have given us
a place in the world and in your work.
Amen.

From the known to the unknown

Do the children know anybody who's scared of spiders? It's amazing how often big, strong people can be reduced to jelly by something much smaller and weaker than they are!

Tell the story: 1 Samuel 17:1-54

(See page 27 for a dramatised version of this story.)

The Bigger They Come . . .

The battlefield was ready. The armies were facing each other across a valley, the Israelites on one hill and their greatest enemies, the Philistines, on the one opposite. Everyone was nervous, wondering who would start the battle, when out of the Philistine camp came the biggest man anyone had ever seen. Even the mountain looked smaller, when he was on it.

'Well, who's going to fight me?'

Goliath's voice echoed horribly from hill to hill and back again, while the Israelite soldiers looked at one another as if to say, 'Not me, mate!' You couldn't blame them. The man was nearly three metres tall – and two would have been quite enough. The armour he was wearing weighed fifty-seven kilograms, which is about as much as a small man or a boy, and that was without counting his helmet. In his hand he'd got this spear that looked like a rugby post, and the big metal point fixed to the top of it weighed as much as seven bags of sugar. Well, would you have taken him on? Exactly. Neither would I.

He wasn't taking 'No' for an answer, though. 'What are you all doing over there?' he yelled. 'Come on, send one man to fight me. If he kills me you can have the rest of the army as slaves. But if *I* win – and I rather think I will – then you'll be doing *our* chores for us. Well? Come on – I dare you.'

As Goliath's voice died away, the only sound to be heard in the valley was a strange clattering noise – Israelite knees knocking together with fear. Every soldier was praying, 'Please, God, don't ask me to fight him!' Then they heard a different voice.

'What's his game, then? Who does he think he is? Cheek, I call it, talking to us like that – it's an insult to God, that's what it is! Someone ought to teach him a lesson.' The speaker was young David, the shepherd boy who had come to bring some food to his brothers who were in the army. 'I'll do it,' he went on. 'I'll show that great big pile of mushroom compost that he can't talk to us like that.'

It was probably a good thing the soldiers were so scared, or they might have died laughing. 'You,' one of them said, 'teach *him*? Teach him what? Embroidery?'

In at least one way, David was very like Goliath – he was full of talk, too! 'I tell you, I can do it – I'm not afraid of him.' Well, eventually they took him to King Saul, and he couldn't shut him up, either. 'I've faced worse than him,' he said. 'I've fought wolves, I've rescued lambs from roaring lions, I've killed hyenas, I've –'

'OK, OK,' Saul protested. 'I give in. You'd better borrow my armour, though – I don't think that bit of old sheepskin's going to protect you, unless the smell of it drives Goliath away.'

David tried the armour, but it was no good. 'I'll be quicker on my feet without it. If God can protect me from lions and wolves, I don't need armour against that windbag out there.' And he went. Just like that.

As he crossed the valley, he stopped at the stream, chose five smooth pebbles for ammunition and got his sling at the ready. It was a drill he knew well – all that talk about wolves and lions wasn't *just* talk.

Goliath went ballistic when he saw David. 'Is this somebody's idea of a joke,' he bellowed, 'a boy coming to throw stones at me? I'll teach you to mess with Goliath. I'll tear you limb from limb! I'll vivisect you! When I've finished with you the vultures will think it's Christmas – whatever that is!' With that, Goliath raised his great spear and aimed it at David.

Goliath knew all about fighting. He knew the rules about how to throw a spear, and how to thrust a sword. But there were some things they didn't teach you at the military academy – and the last thing he expected was a stone between the eyes. The *very* last thing he expected . . .

Goliath had never been good at thinking, talking and acting at the same time. So he was fully occupied, shouting his insult, thinking of his next one and aiming his spear, and he simply hadn't got a brain-cell to spare. So he didn't notice David putting a stone into his sling and swinging it round his head. The stone hit him, smack in the middle of his forehead, just as his spear arm was at full stretch. What happened next was a slow-motion action sequence that any cameraman would have been proud of. Perfectly balanced, with his arm locked above his head, Goliath seemed to take a little time for the fact that he was dead to sink in. Then, slowly, his grip relaxed and the massive spear hit the ground just as his knees gave way and his huge body teetered and fell.

Well, things got a bit wild after that, with celebrations and parties – and a few more things I'd rather not tell you about because they were extremely not-very-nice, and quite unnecessary. David went on to become a great king, which only goes to show that size isn't everything.

Respond to the story

Discussion

Why did the soldiers not take David seriously?

- Because he was so young?
- Because he was small?
- Because he was not a trained fighter?
- All three?
- Any other ideas?

Song

One or more of the following songs might be used here and/or in the all-age worship:

Goliath was big and Goliath was strong
Jesus is greater than the greatest heroes
Think big: an elephant
When the Spirit of the Lord is within my heart
Whether you're one or whether you're two

Art and craft

✔ Make a large (ideally, life-size) painting of Goliath, either on a board or several large pieces of paper joined together. (See 'Word and action' in the all-age worship for how this would be used.) You will also need some 'stone' cards for the congregation to write on. Obviously they need to be somewhat bigger than real pebbles to allow for this – about the diameter of a tea cup would be good. Cut them out of buff card and set them aside for the service. Between now and then, find some local power issues, e.g. the closure of a school or hospital that people value, or the loss of a vital bus service. If you can't find anything suitable, then a use a fictitious example such as one of those.

Draw or paint a picture of David fighting Goliath.

This is the key picture, but you might want to do others in addition to it, such as:

- Goliath issuing his challenge from the mountain
- David arguing with King Saul
- David sorting out the stones in the brook

Drama: The Bigger They Come

Narrator	The battlefield was ready. The armies were facing each other across a valley, the Israelites on one hill and their greatest enemies, the Philistines, opposite. Everyone was wondering who would start, when out of the Philistine camp came an enormous man. Even the mountain looked smaller, when he was on it.
Goliath	Well, who's going to fight me?
Narrator	Goliath was nearly three metres tall. His armour weighed fifty-seven kilograms, which is about as much as a small man or a boy, and that was without counting his helmet. He'd got this spear that looked like a rugby post, and the big metal point fixed to the top of it weighed as much as seven bags of sugar. Well, would you have taken him on? Exactly. Neither would I.
Goliath	What are you all doing over there? Come on, send one man to fight me. If he kills me you can have the rest of our army as slaves, but if *I* win – and I rather think I will – then you'll be doing *our* chores for us. Well? Come on – I dare you.
Narrator	As Goliath's voice died away, the only sound to be heard in the valley was a strange clattering noise – Israelite knees knocking together with fear! Every solider was praying, 'Please, God, don't ask me to fight him!' Then they heard a different voice.
David	What's his game, then? Who does he think he is? It's an insult to God. Someone ought to teach him a lesson.
Narrator	The speaker was young David, the shepherd boy who had come to bring some food to his brothers who were in the army.
David	I'll do it. I'll show that great big pile of mushroom compost that he can't talk to us like that.
First soldier	You? Don't be silly!*
Second soldier	
Third soldier	
David	I tell you, I can do it – I'm not afraid of him.
Narrator	Well, eventually they took him to King Saul, and he couldn't shut him up, either.
David	I've faced worse than him. I've faced hungry wolves, I've rescued lambs from the very jaws of roaring lions, I've killed hyenas, I've –

* You may like to write in some of the things the children said during the discussion.

Saul OK, OK, I give in. You'd better borrow my armour, though – I don't think that bit of old sheepskin's going to protect you, unless the smell of it drives Goliath away.

Narrator David tried the armour, but it was no good.

David It'll only slow me down. If God can protect me from lions and wolves, I don't need armour against that windbag out there.

Narrator As he crossed the valley, he stopped at the stream, chose five smooth pebbles for ammunition and got his sling at the ready. It was a drill he knew well – all that talk about wolves and lions wasn't just talk. Goliath went ballistic when he saw David.

Goliath Is this somebody's idea of a joke, a boy coming to throw stones at me? I'll teach you to mess with Goliath. I'll tear you limb from limb! I'll vivisect you! When I've finished with you the vultures will think it's Christmas – whatever that is!

Narrator With that, Goliath raised his great spear and aimed it at David. Goliath knew all about how to throw a spear, and how to thrust a sword. But he'd never been good at thinking, talking and acting at the same time. So he was fully occupied, shouting his insult, thinking of his next one and aiming his spear, and he simply hadn't got a brain-cell to spare. He didn't notice David putting a stone into his sling and swinging it round. The stone hit him, smack in the middle of his forehead, just as his spear arm was at full stretch. Goliath seemed to take a little time for the fact that he was dead to sink in. Then, slowly, his grip relaxed and the massive spear hit the ground just as his knees gave way and his huge body teetered and fell. Well, things got a bit wild after that, with celebrations and parties – and a few more things I'd rather not tell you about because they were extremely not-very-nice, and quite unnecessary. David went on to become a great king, which only goes to show that size isn't everything.

David needs five stones that won't snag in his sling. Colour the best ones so that they're easier to find.

Help David to get to Goliath, passing the stream on the way.

WORDSEARCH

Find the following words in the grid:
DAVID, GOLIATH, SAUL, PHILISTINE, ISRAELITE, STONES, SLING, SPEAR, ARMOUR, MOUNTAIN, GIANT, SHEPHERD

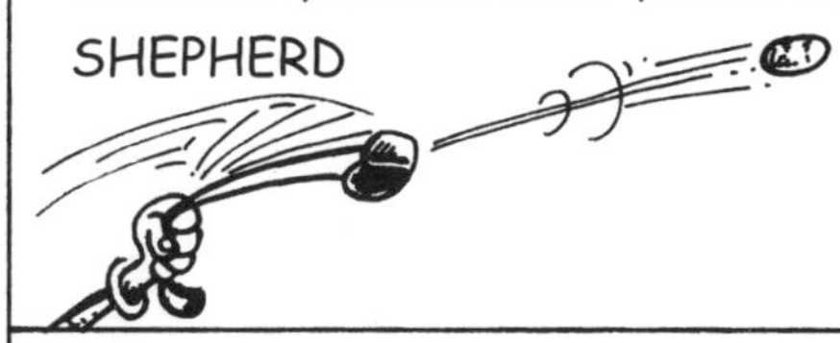

D	A	P	H	I	L	I	S	T	I	N	E
H	G	I	A	N	U	N	I	L	S	A	S
M	O	U	N	T	A	I	N	P	R	R	H
S	L	I	N	T	S	P	E	E	A	M	E
G	I	A	N	G	I	A	N	A	E	O	P
D	A	V	I	D	R	D	B	R	L	U	H
A	T	G	N	U	L	S	X	S	I	T	E
T	H	F	O	Z	S	E	N	O	T	S	R
I	N	M	O	L	N	V	S	N	E	P	D
D	R	A	I	G	O	L	A	E	T	E	A
A	G	N	I	C	T	O	J	S	Y	A	V
X	G	C	V	G	S	W	I	N	G	T	I

Week 3: David and Bathsheba

Thinking about it

What's the point?

The trouble is that even the little things we do can have big consequences, and we have no way of predicting them – so we need to be on the look-out for things getting out of hand. Even God's most special people can get into that kind of mess sometimes – but he can still use them. We need to try to avoid doing bad things, but at least we know that if God could still work with David after the dreadful thing he did then he can still love and use us when we make (hopefully rather smaller) mistakes.

Doing it

Prayer

Loving God,
thank you for being with us,
and staying with us even when we get things wrong.
Thank you for helping us to learn and to begin again.
Please bless all that we do together today,
and help us to know that you are enjoying our time together, too. Amen.

From the known to the unknown

Have some dominoes set up end to end in a row. Let a few of the children take it in turns to tip one over so that all the others are knocked down. Life's a bit like that. One thing leads to another, and sometimes a quite small thing we do can end up having big effects. The story today is about how even the great King David made a really silly mistake that eventually got completely out of hand. By the time it was over a lot of people had been hurt. But the good news is that, although he couldn't undo the harm he'd done, and although he himself got badly hurt by it, God still loved him and still made him into a great king.

Tell the story: 2 Samuel 11:1-12:13

(See page 33 for a dramatised version of this story.)

One Thing Leads to Another

David had come a long way since he threw that famous stone at Goliath. He'd become king – but that doesn't mean throwing stones is a good idea, mind you. Anyway, he was living in his palace, with lots of servants all doing what he told them and no one at all to tell *him* what to do. Or so he thought. So he began to think he could do whatever he liked – and people who think *that* usually end up hurting others or getting hurt themselves. David managed to do both.

He was up on his roof one afternoon (a flat roof with a safety rail, so don't *you* go getting ideas) when he realised he could see into the window of a nearby house. His first mistake was to carry on looking instead of turning away like a good, well-brought-up king. What he saw was a very beautiful woman taking a bath – at which point of course he most certainly should have looked away. Instead, he called a servant.

'Er, would you happen to know who lives in that house over there? You know, the one with the potted palms on the balcony? No? Well, find out for me, will you?'

The servant did just that, and reported back to the king. 'That's Uriah's house,' he said, 'but he's away in the army, fighting in the war. There's just his wife, Bathsheba, living there at the moment.'

'Oh, what a shame – she must be really lonely without Uriah there,' David thought. 'And I know just the person to cheer her up. Me.'

David was going to do a very bad thing, and he should have stopped right there – but he didn't. He invited Bathsheba round, and they became very good friends. And it wasn't long before Bathsheba started to love David more than she loved her own husband. One day, she told David she had some news for him.

'We're going to have a baby,' she said.

David knew that when Uriah found out he would be really angry – and it's not the sort of thing you can keep secret. David certainly didn't want a big scandal at the palace, so he had to think of a way out. And that's when things got *really* out of hand.

David sent a message to General Joab at the battle front. 'I want you to put Uriah right at the front of the next charge,' he said. 'Then I want you all to move away and leave him surrounded by enemy soldiers.' Now you can see that David had really lost the plot as far as the difference between right and wrong goes. And to think it had all started out with a sneaky look through a bathroom window!

The plan worked. Uriah got killed, and they had a big memorial service for him where David cried a lot and said how sorry he was to lose such a good soldier and friend. Then David and Bathsheba got married.

David thought because he was king no one would dare to question what he'd done. But he was wrong. It wasn't long before he got a surprise visitor.

'Hello, Nathan, how's my favourite prophet today?'

Nathan looked serious. 'There's been a terrible injustice' he said.

'Tell me,' said David, grandly. 'You know I always care about injustice.'

Nathan knew he had to be clever – you can't just come straight out and tell a ruthless, powerful dictator that he's a grade one wrong-un, now can you? He had to get David on his side first.

'Well, Your Majesty,' he said, 'it's about two men, one rich and the other poor. The rich man had lots of animals – cattle, sheep, everything, and the poor man had just this one little lamb that he loved.'

David could hear a really good story coming on, so he made himself comfortable. 'Go on, Nathan?'

'Thank you. One night the rich man had a visitor, and he was too mean to kill one of his own animals to give his friend dinner, so he stole the poor man's lamb, killed it and served it up as if it were his own.'

David was hopping mad. 'He dies!' he shouted. 'But not before he's paid back four times as much as he stole. Who is he? TELL ME WHO HE IS!'

Well, he had asked for it, hadn't he? 'It's you, Your Majesty,' said Nathan. 'After all that God's done for you, taking you from that cold, draughty hill-side where you minded sheep and making you king of Israel, you go and do that horrible thing to Uriah.'

David suddenly realised what he had done – and he was terribly, terribly sorry. He cried, and he prayed, but of course he couldn't actually change the past, however much he tried to.

David learnt an important lesson from that. And because he learnt, God helped him to become a good king – even though not a perfect one.

Respond to the story

Discussion

Can the children see how the thing spiralled out of control? What were the critical points where David could have stopped things getting worse?

- By turning away the first time he saw into Bathsheba's window?
- By not inviting her round?
- By making sure they stayed just good friends?
- By telling Uriah the truth and apologising?

Song

One or more of the following songs might be used here and/or in the all-age worship:

God's love is deeper than the deepest ocean
I'm accepted, I'm forgiven
It's me, it's me, it's me, O Lord
Jesus put this song into our hearts
Make me a channel of your peace
Never let Jesus into your heart

Art and craft

✔ Do a large painting of King David. (See 'Word and action' in the all-age worship for how this would be used.) This could be either head-and-shoulders or full length if you prefer, but leave space either side to write things up at the service. Draw a vertical line straight down the centre, and put the heading 'Good' at one side, and 'Bad' at the other.

Draw or paint a picture of Uriah lying dead on the ground.

This is the key picture, but you might want to do others in addition to it, such as:

- David writing a letter to Joab
- Nathan telling David off
- David praying for forgiveness

Drama: One Thing Leads to Another

Narrator King David was living in his palace, with lots of servants all doing what he told them and no one at all to tell *him* what to do. Or so he thought. So he began to think he could do whatever he liked – and people who think *that* usually end up hurting others or getting hurt themselves. David managed to do both. One afternoon, he realised he could see into the window of a nearby house. His first mistake was to carry on looking instead of turning away like a good, well-brought-up king. What he saw was a very beautiful woman taking a bath – at which point of course he most *certainly* should have looked away. Instead, he called a servant.

David Er, would you happen to know who lives in that house over there? You know, the one with the potted palms on the balcony?

Servant I'm afraid I don't know, Your Majesty.

David Well, find out for me, will you?

Narrator The servant did just that, and reported back to the king.

Servant That's Uriah's house, but he's away in the army, fighting in the war. There's just his wife Bathsheba living there at the moment.

David Oh, what a shame – she must be really lonely without Uriah there. [*Aside*] And I know just the person to cheer her up. Me.

Narrator David was going to do a very bad thing, and he should have stopped right there – but he didn't. He invited Bathsheba round, and they became very good friends – and more.

Bathsheba You know, David, I think I love you more than my own husband.

Narrator Now, things should *definitely* have stopped at that point, but they didn't – and soon Bathsheba had news for David.

Bathsheba We're going to have a baby.

David That's torn it! Uriah will be really angry – and it's not something you can keep secret. I don't want a big scandal at the palace.

Narrator David had to find a way out. And that's when things got really out of hand. He sent a message to General Joab at the battle front.

David I want you to put Uriah right at the front of the next charge. Then move away and leave him surrounded by enemy soldiers.

Narrator Now you can see that David had really lost the plot as far as the difference between right and wrong goes. And to think it had all started out with a sneaky look through a bathroom window! Uriah got killed, and they had a big memorial service for him where David cried a lot and said how sorry he was to lose such a good soldier and friend. Then David and Bathsheba got married.

David I'm the king – no one would dare to question what I've done.

Narrator He was wrong. It wasn't long before he got a surprise visitor.

David Hello, Nathan, how's my favourite prophet today?

Nathan There's been a terrible injustice.

David Tell me. You know I always care about injustice.

Nathan [*Aside*] I've got to be clever – I can't just come straight out and tell a ruthless, powerful dictator that he's a grade one wrong-un, now can I? I've got to get David on side first. [*To David*] Well, Your Majesty, it's about two men, one rich and the other poor. The rich man had lots of animals – cattle, sheep, everything – and the poor man had just this one little lamb that he loved. One night the rich man had a visitor, and he was too mean to kill one of his own animals to give his friend dinner, so he stole the poor man's lamb, killed it and served it up as if it were his own.

David [*Angrily*] He dies! But not before he's paid back four times as much as he stole. Who is he? TELL ME WHO HE IS!

Nathan It's you. After all that God's done for you, taking you from that cold, draughty hillside where you minded sheep and making you king of Israel, you go and do that horrible thing to Uriah.

Narrator David suddenly realised what he had done – and he was terribly sorry. He cried, and he prayed, but of course he couldn't actually change the past, however much he tried to. David learnt an important lesson from that. And because he learnt, God helped him to become a good king – even though not a perfect one.

David is looking into Bathsheba's window – and he's going to regret it!
Can you see some less dangerous things for him to look at?

Crack the code

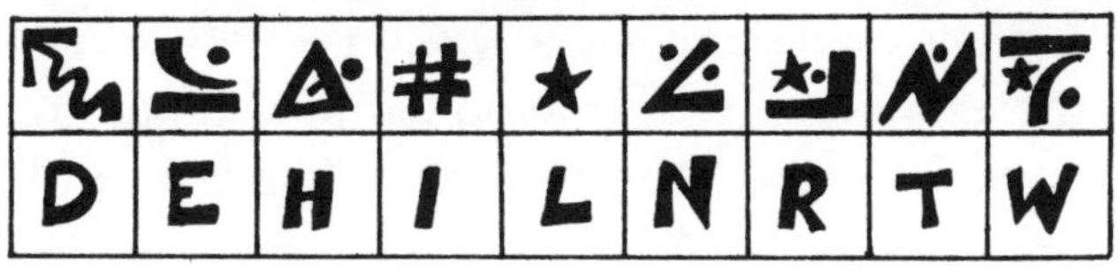

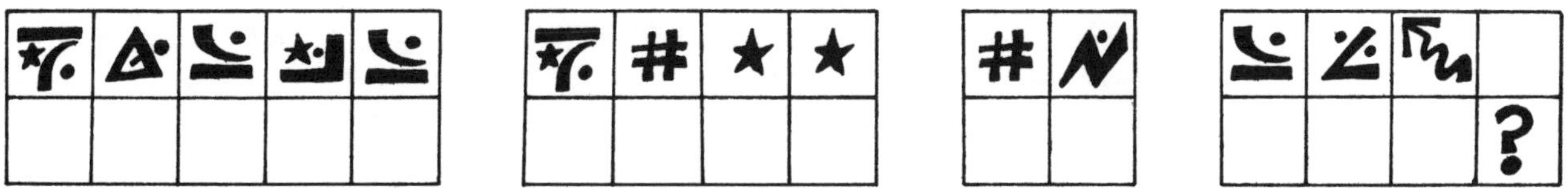

Tick the good ways of getting to know our neighbours.

WORDSEARCH

Find the following words in the grid:

DAVID, BATHSHEBA, NATHAN, URIAH, JOAB, SCANDAL, INJUSTICE, WINDOW, ROOF, BATHROOM, RIGHT, WRONG, POWER.

D	A	V	E	D	A	C	A	H	T	A	N
R	I	G	B	A	T	H	S	H	E	B	A
I	L	R	A	V	I	N	J	U	S	T	H
G	A	E	T	I	U	R	I	A	W	A	T
H	D	W	J	D	M	A	N	A	I	N	A
S	N	O	R	O	O	F	J	R	N	A	N
E	A	P	O	W	O	R	U	R	D	A	H
B	C	A	N	D	R	I	S	U	O	T	J
C	S	N	A	T	H	G	T	N	W	R	O
S	C	A	N	D	T	R	I	G	H	T	A
W	R	O	N	G	A	S	C	A	N	D	P
B	A	T	H	R	B	O	E	J	O	A	S

Week 4: All-age worship

Opening song

A song praising and celebrating the faithfulness of God

Welcome and statement of the theme

Get one or more of the children to point out or hold up the pictures as you sum up the story (breaking off from this suggested summary as necessary, in order to include the particular pictures, etc., the children have produced).

In Junior Church during the past few weeks, we've been learning about King David: about how God chose him when he was just a rather unimpressive shepherd boy and had him anointed as king to take over from Saul; about how when he was still only a boy he fought with the giant Goliath and saved Israel from defeat; but we've also learnt about how even this great man went sadly wrong when he fell in love with Uriah's wife, Bathsheba – one wrong thing led to another until he ended up committing murder. But even then God was still able to use David, show him what he'd done wrong and make him into a great king of Israel.

That's the general picture, but today we're going to concentrate on: [*Name the episode of your choice*]

Prayer

– use whichever is appropriate

Based on Week 1

Loving God,
we thank you for knowing us so well,
and loving us as we are.
Forgive us for the times we make snap judgements about people,
based on just what little we know,
and especially when we shut people out
because of those judgements.
Help us to love people the way you love them. Amen.

Based on Week 2

Loving God,
we're here to celebrate your goodness
and especially your concern for justice.
Thank you for being a God who cares,
and forgive us for the apathy we sometimes show,
especially when faced with big, powerful organisations.
Help us always to care about people
who need someone to speak for them,
and to show them your love. Amen.

Based on Week 3

Holy God,
we're here to celebrate your goodness and your love.
Thank you for making us the way we are,
with such potential for greatness.
Please forgive us for the times we misuse the power we have –
especially for the little selfish things we sometimes do
without realising the greater harm they might lead to.
Remind us again of your love,
and give us assurance of your forgiveness,
through Jesus Christ our Lord.
Amen.

Word and action – use whichever is appropriate

From Week 1

Bring the three monarchs to the front, and let them put on their crowns. Explain to the congregation that they can choose which is going to be king/queen by listening to what they would do if they were chosen. The catch is that one of them isn't telling the truth. But which one? Let the children read out their manifestos or, if they prefer, get someone to read for them. Then divide the congregation into groups to play a kind of royal 'Call My Bluff'. They have to decide which monarch they're going to choose and since they've got no indication as to which one is 'lying', they're going to have to go on outward appearances only. Divide them into groups to discuss and make their choices. If they want to be reminded of the manifestos you can give each group a photocopy of each card. After a suitable time, ask each group whom they have chosen. Ask the children to open their cards and reveal who is the bad monarch.

Now read the story, either in narrative or drama form.

From Week 2

Put up the large picture of Goliath before the service and have the cards ready. Read the story, either in drama or narrative form, and ask the congregation what 'Goliath' might represent for them – you've got your own ideas already lined up in case you need them – and write up one or more of their suggestions in big writing around Goliath's head. Now divide the congregation into groups. If there are several issues written up you could designate one for each group – otherwise they can all discuss the same one. The question is, what can they do about it? What kind of 'stones' can these apparently powerless people throw at 'Goliath'? Ask them to write the things they think of on their 'stone' cards. As they're discussing things, wander round keeping your ears open for any groups that are struggling, so that you can possibly give them one or two pointers. Examples might be: writing to the newspapers or to their MP; getting up a petition; taking part in a demonstration; joining a protest group; raising awareness by an event at church . . .

After an appropriate time, call the groups back to order and ask some people from each group to say what they have written on their stones, and then come and pin or stick them onto the picture of Goliath. It doesn't matter if (as is virtually inevitable) several groups have thought of the same thing – the more there are, the more effective their action might be.

Then look at the beleaguered Goliath and simply observe that we're not as impotent as we may think in the face of the abuse of power.

From Week 3

Read the story, either in drama or narrative form. Put up the large picture of David and invite the congregation to brainstorm some 'good' and 'bad' names for David.

'Good' might include such titles as 'Righter of wrongs', 'Brave Soldier', 'Caring Shepherd', 'Hymn writer' (you may or may not think that a good title, but I couldn't possibly comment!).

'Bad' might include 'Liar', 'Adulterer', 'Murderer'.

Ask the congregation: could these really be the same person?

All of us are mixtures of good and bad – so we need to be a bit careful how we judge others (whether we put them on high pedestals from which they're bound to fall, or label them as bad or worse and assume there can be no good in them).

Song 2

Offering

This may be introduced as a small thing we offer to God that he can take and use for great things in his world.

Offertory prayer

Thank you, Lord, for using whatever we offer,
however small or however imperfect it may be.
Take and use these gifts
so that more people may know of your love.
Through Jesus Christ our Lord.
Amen.

Song 3

Reading

Matthew 21:14-16 read from a standard Bible. Introduce it with words such as: In our Bible reading, Jesus reminds us of the importance of what may seem too small to matter.

Talk (optional)

If you feel it appropriate (and if time permits) you could talk about how Jesus valued the love of small children, and said that their praise was accepted by God. Isn't that part of what all-age worship is about? In this service we haven't just 'given the children something to do', but have taken their offerings and made them the basis of joyful worship that was satisfying to us and infinitely worthy to God. Let's never devalue the importance of what seems small – and inevitably is less than perfect!

Notices and family news

Prayers of intercession

These could be led entirely by the minister or other adult(s), and/or could include some prayers written by the children themselves – or simply some points that they have raised in discussion.

Song 4

Closing prayer/benediction

Unit 2
Solomon – called to be wise

Overview of the unit

We take three key events:

Week 1: Solomon becomes king

Here we see Solomon becoming king, fighting off the challenge from the scheming Adonijah, and praying for that vital quality of leadership: wisdom.

Week 2: Solomon's wise judgement

Solomon's wisdom is put to the test, and his famous judgement shows that simply 'knowing right from wrong', however important, is not always enough. Wisdom is something much deeper than mere knowledge.

Week 3: Solomon builds the temple

The climax of Solomon's reign: the building of the temple. Solomon's wisdom shows both in the way he organised the building work and in the prayer he offered at the dedication of the temple.

All-age worship

Here you may choose to focus on any one of the three subthemes, but place it in the context of the overall story and theme: Solomon's wise kingship. So while the specific theme chosen will be emphasised in the choice of 'Word and action' material, some of the art and craft work the children have done in the other weeks will be used to decorate the church and set the context of the wider story.

Important note

✔ The ticked activities in Weeks 1-3 are intended as the link material for the 'Word and action' slot in the all-age worship. You will only need to do this in one of the three weeks – depending on which week's subtheme is going to be the main emphasis in the service.

Week 1: Solomon becomes king

Thinking about it

What's the point?

Solomon's choice of wisdom as the gift he most desired from God sets him apart from Adonijah whose ambition clearly clouded his judgement – eventually with fatal consequences. It was Solomon's wisdom, not Adonijah's self-serving cleverness, that Israel needed at that turbulent moment in history.

Doing it

Prayer

Loving God,
thank you for bringing us together in this place.
Please join in the things we do this morning,
and help us to learn more about you
and to remember how much you love us. Amen.

From the known to the unknown

Have a few well-known items the children are likely to purchase frequently – sweets, comics, that sort of thing – and ask them if they can tell you the prices of them. Congratulate them when they get it right – 'I'd enjoy shopping with you, you're really on the ball, aren't you!'

Then produce a box labelled '1 Kilo Common Sense' and ask if anyone knows the price of that. Enjoy the banter this may well start off, and then point out that there are some things you can't buy – but they're the most valuable of all.

Tell the story

(See page 46 for a dramatised version of this story.)

Two Kings, a Queen and a Knave

There was just one thing everyone in Israel wanted to know: who would be their next king? Well, King David was getting old, and no one lives for ever, do they? The trouble was that King David had lots of sons – and quite a few of them wanted to be the next king – and some of them weren't too fussy about how they did it.

Adonijah was just one of them. He knew that his father hadn't chosen him, so he had to be clever. He chose some of his friends, including a priest called Abiathar to do the coronation, and had a big ceremony. He said lots of prayers (because the people wouldn't want a king who wasn't religious) and had himself proclaimed the new king of Israel. 'That should fix it,' he thought. 'By the time Dad finds out, he'll be dead anyway and it'll be too late to do anything about it. I've done it! I'm the king! I'm the man! Boy, but does a bit of power feel good!'

The trouble was, Adonijah had forgotten about Nathan the prophet. Nathan didn't miss much – and he was a very good friend of David. And he knew David wanted Solomon to be king – not Adonijah.

Nathan went to see Bathsheba, who was Solomon's mother, and told her what had happened. Bathsheba knew if Adonijah were king she and Solomon wouldn't be safe – he'd kill the pair of them to make sure he was in control. 'We've got to stop him,' Nathan said. 'Now, here's the plan . . .'

Bathsheba went into David's room. He was very old, very ill and she knew she had no time to lose. She bowed very low – even the king's wife had to remember the ceremonial – and said, 'Remember how you promised that Solomon would be king after you? Well, Adonijah's gone and told everybody *he's* the new king. He had this big ceremony – funny he never mentioned it to any of us, don't you think?'

Right on cue, Nathan came into the room. 'Your Majesty,' he said, 'I'm sorry to bother you, but did you agree to Adonijah becoming king? I just thought I ought to check, that's all – because he's swanning around in a crown and a big smug smile and making everyone say "Your Majesty". Just thought you ought to know in case you'd OK'd it and forgotten to tell me, you know.'

'I did nothing of the sort,' gasped David. (In earlier days he'd probably have bellowed, but he was on his deathbed, so you have to make allowances.) 'Go and get Solomon, and get a decent priest – Zadok will do – we've got a coronation to organise.'

So Zadok was sent for, and he anointed Solomon as king, and they made sure that everyone knew this was what David wanted. Very soon, people were singing and dancing, and shouting that Solomon was king, and how he was going to be even greater than David.

Meanwhile, Adonijah was celebrating. But just as he was getting used to his new crown, who should walk in but Jonathan – the son of the priest who'd just anointed him – and he had bad news.

'I think you should know that your father's made Solomon king – big ceremony, publicity, the works.'

'Oh, my word – that's me finished, then. Solomon'll kill me!' Adonijah did what a lot of people do when they're in trouble – he prayed. Before long, word got to Solomon that Adonijah was terrified.

'Tell him not to worry,' said Solomon. 'I won't hurt him as long as he behaves himself – but if ever I get the idea he's plotting against me, he's dead. Right?'

Meanwhile, David wasn't getting any better. He sent for Solomon and said, 'I know I'm dying, so it's over to you, now. Be a good king, won't you? Listen to God and do what he wants you to – then I know the people will be OK with you in charge. Oh, and don't take any nonsense: there are a few people you need to watch – you know what to do about them.'

A little bit later, God spoke to Solomon in a dream. 'Is there anything particular you'd like me to give you?' he asked.

Solomon answered, 'Well, you were really good to my dad when he was alive, and now I've got to try and be as good a king as he was. You know, a little bit of wisdom wouldn't go amiss. I want to be a good king and help my people to be happy. Yes, I reckon a spot of wisdom would do nicely.

God was impressed. No, I mean seriously impressed. 'You could have asked for anything,' he said, 'long life, money – but you asked for wisdom.

So I'll tell you what I'm going to do. I'm going to give you money as well – just as a kind of extra. And you'll be famous, too – don't get carried away by it, but it's a nice touch.'

God kept his word. Solomon got the wisdom he'd prayed for, and became a really great king.

And what about Adonijah? Well, to cut a long story short, he forgot Solomon's warning, got big ideas again and completely lost his head, if you see what I mean. It's a pity *he* didn't pray for wisdom, too – isn't it?

Respond to the story

Discussion

What other things could Solomon have asked God for?

- Money?
- An easy life?
- Power?

Why did they need a priest to anoint a new king?

- Because it was traditional and looked good?
- Because otherwise the people wouldn't accept him?
- Because God was the *real* 'king' in Israel?

Song

One or more of the following songs might be used here and/or in the all-age worship:

I'm gonna click
Seek ye first the kingdom of God
This little light of mine
Who's the king of the jungle

Art and craft

✔ Make some models and/or pictures of luxury goods – cardboard boxes can be turned into video players, cameras, TV sets, computers, etc., and the children will certainly be able to think of others. (See 'Word and action' in the all-age worship for how this would be used.) Decide a price for each item and write it on a price ticket for the leader to have at the service. Add to the selection the box of wisdom (common sense) you used earlier in the session and have ready a ticket marked 'Absolutely Priceless'. Make sure the children understand why they're doing this: these things all have a high price, but they're not as valuable as the things God can give us for free – and together you're going to teach that to the Church!

Draw or paint a picture of Solomon at prayer.

This is the key picture, but you might want to do others in addition to it, such as:

- Solomon being anointed by Zadok and Nathan
- Bathsheba talking to David
- David on his bed, blessing Solomon

Drama: Two Kings, a Queen and a Knave

Narrator Everyone in Israel wanted to know who would be their next king. King David was getting old, and the trouble was that he had lots of sons, and quite a few of them wanted to be king – and some weren't fussy about how they did it. Like Adonijah, for example.

Adonijah I know my father's chosen Solomon, but I'll get a few friends and a priest – Abiathar will do – and get myself crowned first. By the time Dad finds out, he'll be dead and it'll be too late.

Narrator The trouble was, Adonijah had forgotten about Nathan the prophet. Nathan didn't miss much – and he was a good friend of David. And he knew David wanted Solomon to be king – not Adonijah. So he went to warn Bathsheba, who was Solomon's mother.

Bathsheba This is awful! If Adonijah becomes king, Solomon and I won't be safe – he'll kill the pair of us to make sure he's in control.

Nathan We've got to stop him. Now, here's the plan . . .

Narrator Bathsheba went into David's room. He was very old, very ill and she knew she had no time to lose. She bowed very low – even the king's wife had to remember the ceremonial.

Bathsheba Remember how you promised that Solomon would be king after you? Well, Adonijah's gone and told everybody *he's* the new king. He had this big ceremony – funny he never mentioned it to any of us, don't you think?

Narrator Right on cue, Nathan came into the room.

Nathan Your Majesty, I'm sorry to intrude, but did you agree to Adonijah becoming king? I just thought I ought to check, that's all – because he's swanning around in a crown and a big smug smile and making everyone say 'Your Majesty'. Just thought you ought to know in case you'd OK'd it and forgotten to tell me, you know.

David I did nothing of the sort. Go and get Solomon, and get a decent priest – Zadok will do – we've got a *real* coronation to organise.

Narrator So Zadok was sent for, and he anointed Solomon as king, and they made sure that everyone knew this was what David wanted. Soon, people were singing and dancing, and shouting about how Solomon was going to be even greater than David. Meanwhile, Adonijah was celebrating. But just as he was getting used to his new crown, who should walk in but Jonathan – the son of the priest who'd just anointed him – and he had bad news.

Jonathan I think you should know that your father's made Solomon king – big ceremony, publicity, the works.

Adonijah Oh, my word – that's me finished, then. Solomon'll kill me! Well, only one thing to do when you're desperate – let's pray!

Narrator Before long, word got to Solomon that Adonijah was terrified.

Solomon Tell him I won't hurt him as long as he behaves himself – but if ever I get the idea he's plotting against me, he's dead. Right?

Narrator Meanwhile, David wasn't getting any better. He sent for Solomon.

David I know I'm dying. Be a good king. Listen to God and do what he says – then I know the people will be OK with you in charge.

Narrator A little bit later, God spoke to Solomon in a dream.

God Is there anything particular you'd like me to give you?

Solomon Let's see. I could ask for*

or perhaps

or maybe

No, I know what I want. You were really good to my dad when he was alive, and now I've got to try and be as good a king as he was. What about some wisdom? I want my people to be happy. Yes, a spot of wisdom would do nicely.

God I'm impressed. No, I mean seriously impressed. You could have asked for money – but you asked for wisdom. I'm going to give you money as well – just as a kind of extra. And you'll be famous, too – don't get carried away by it, but it's a nice touch.

Narrator God kept his word. Solomon got the wisdom he'd prayed for, and became a really great king. And what about Adonijah? Well, to cut a long story short, he forgot Solomon's warning, got big ideas again and completely lost his head, if you see what I mean. It's a pity *he* didn't pray for wisdom, too – isn't it?

* Here you could insert some of the things the children thought of earlier.

Which hat will Solomon choose?
Which one best suits Adonijah?

I will give you wisdom. (1 Kings 3:12)

Unscramble these words and fit them in the grid. If you get it right, Solomon's prayer will show in the middle box.

EWTALH, NAOHDJIA, VDDAI, TBHASBHEA, AZKDO, LSOMOON.

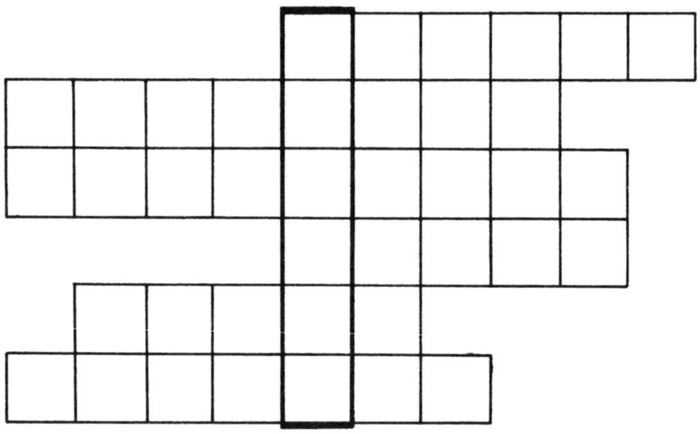

A	D	O	N	I	J	A	M	G	O	F	G
A	Z	A	D	O	N	I	J	A	T	H	A
V	A	D	O	N	M	A	T	H	S	H	E
I	K	W	I	S	A	O	M	L	O	S	A
G	O	D	A	B	I	T	L	O	M	O	W
A	D	O	N	I	J	A	H	O	S	I	I
B	A	T	H	S	H	E	B	A	S	A	S
I	Z	A	O	D	I	V	A	D	N	O	D
A	B	I	A	T	H	A	O	O	L	M	O
T	O	L	O	M	O	M	I	D	A	V	M
H	W	I	S	D	O	N	A	T	H	A	C
A	A	B	I	A	T	H	A	R	H	M	S

WORDSEARCH
Find the following words in the grid:
GOD, SOLOMON, ADONIJAH, DAVID, BATHSHEBA, WISDOM, ANOINT, NATHAN, ZADOK, ABIATHAR.

Week 2: Solomon's wise judgement

Thinking about it

What's the point?

Wisdom is more than mere knowledge or cleverness – true wisdom is about knowing people, understanding human nature, being able to make good judgements and act in ways that are creative and life-giving. True justice demands wisdom as well as knowledge.

Doing it

Prayer

Thank you, God, for loving us,
and for teaching us to care for each other.
Thank you for this special time we have together,
and help us to learn more about sharing
and about loving each other. Amen.

From the known to the unknown

Have a cardboard box handy, and a number of 'valuables' (they don't need to be literally priceless!) Tell the children you're sorting them out to put in the safe for security, because you don't want to lose them. Go through each item and say why it's a valuable possession. Then say, 'You know, this is a really good idea. Perhaps I ought to put my children/grandchildren in the safe, too – so that no harm comes to them.' Ask if they think it's a good idea. If not, why not? Tease out the point that we can't treat people as possessions. We're called to love them, not simply treasure them! That was something Solomon knew well, because he was a wise king.

Tell the story: 1 Kings 3:16-28

(See page 52 for a dramatised version of this story.)

A Matter of Good Judgement

King Solomon was doing really well. When he asked for wisdom, God had answered his prayer. The important thing was that he didn't just know an awful lot – plenty of people know a lot, but they're not very wise. No, Solomon really had his head screwed on. He understood what was important in life, and he knew what made people tick. And boy, was he glad of that when Suzy and Debs came to see him!

You never heard such a commotion! Suzy was screaming at Debs to give her her baby back, and Debs was calling Suzy a rotten little liar – and a few more things as well, but I'm not going to repeat them.

Solomon eventually got them to calm down and tell him what had happened. It turned out the two women shared a flat, and they'd both recently had babies. Then one night, Debs' baby died and she sneakily swapped them over so that Suzy got the dead one and she had the one that was alive. Well, that was what Suzy said. Debs of course told a different story, and the problem was that neither of them was to be trusted, so who was telling the truth?

Solomon was really worried. 'I've got to be really sure whose baby this is,' he thought. 'Trouble is, I don't know the women and I don't know which one to believe. If only there were some way of finding out . . .'

While Solomon was thinking the two women started arguing again. 'I tell you it's my child!' screamed Debs.

'Rubbish!' yelled Suzy. 'He's mine. Yours died, and you swapped them over. That's the truth of it.'

Suddenly, King Solomon had a brilliant idea. He took the baby from Debs, which was a good idea anyway because the argument was making it cry, and put it on the table in front of him. Then he turned to his servant. 'Go and fetch me a sword,' he said.

Everyone wondered what Solomon was going to do. Nobody liked either Debs or Suzy, but they hadn't done anything to deserve to be killed – but why else would Solomon want a sword?

Eventually the servant came back with a big, sharp sword, and Solomon turned to Debs and Suzy. 'Now, is one of you two going to tell me whose baby this really is?'

'I tell you it's mine,' Suzy cried. 'She swapped them. I'm sorry hers is dead, but she's not having mine!'

'You little liar!' shouted Debs. 'You're just jealous of me – you always have been – and now you want my baby. Well you can't have him!'

Solomon turned to his servant. 'I don't see anything else for it,' he said. 'If we can't find out whose baby this is you'd better cut it in half and give half to each of the women.'

There was a big gasp from the crowd, and then everything went quiet – so quiet you could have heard a caterpillar chewing on a leaf. Surely, he couldn't mean it? What would that achieve? Two dead babies instead of one, and two unhappy mothers? Surely, King Solomon couldn't mean to do it?

The servant looked horrified – he didn't mind chopping off traitors' heads if he was asked to – that was just part of the job – but cutting an innocent little baby in half was something else. Something else indeed! He looked at the mothers, then at the baby, and then at the king. 'You must be joking!' he said.

Solomon wasn't joking. 'I never joke about a thing like this,' he pointed out. 'Just do what I say or it'll be worse for you.'

The servant trembled as he lifted the great sword high into the air. Solomon raised his hand. When he dropped it, the servant would bring the sword down. The crowd was deathly silent.

Debs looked quite calm. 'Sounds fair to me,' she said. 'Half each – and I won't have to watch her drooling over him.'

'No, no, no!' Suzy was getting almost hysterical. 'Give him to her – give him to her – I don't want him to die! Just do anything but that. Let her have him!'

'Put the sword away,' ordered the king, and the servant mopped his brow in relief. Then Solomon turned to Suzy. 'Take your baby home,' he said. 'I can see he's yours because you loved him enough to let him go.'

Suzy took her baby, crying with joy, and Solomon walked back into his palace.

'You didn't think I'd really cut that child in half, did you?' he said to his servant. 'I just had to find out which one really loved him, and which one just wanted him.'

See? I told you Solomon was wise!

Respond to the story

Discussion

Why was Suzy so upset when she saw Solomon's sword?

- Because she cared about her baby?

What was different about Debs?

- She just saw the baby as a possession?

What can we learn from this?

- That loving people means caring about them for their sake, not for what we can get?

Song

One or more of the following songs might be used here and/or in the all-age worship:

A new commandment
Come on and celebrate
Give me oil in my lamp
God made a boomerang
Let love be real*
Let there be love
Make me a channel of your peace

Art and craft

✔ Make a prison cell. (See 'Word and action' in the all-age worship for how this would be used.) A simple barred window made from strips of cardboard will do, or it can be as elaborate as you like.

Draw or paint a picture of the two women with Solomon.

This is the key picture, but you might want to do others in addition to it, such as:

- Suzy finding her dead baby in the cot
- Suzy and Debs arguing
- The servant's sword raised high

* The revised version of this in *21st Century Hymnal* is better than that in the *Children's Hymn Book*.

Drama: A Matter of Good Judgement

Narrator King Solomon was doing really well. When he asked for wisdom, God had answered his prayer. The important thing was that he didn't just *know* an awful lot – plenty of people know a lot, but they're not very wise. No, Solomon really understood what was important in life, and he knew what made people tick. And boy, was he glad of that when Suzy and Debs came to see him!

Suzy You give me my baby back, Debs – right now!

Debs You're mad, Suzy – this is my baby!

Suzy Ooh, you rotten little liar. Ooh, you –

Narrator Bleep, bleep, bleep. Sorry about that, but we can't let her say that here, can we?

Solomon Tell me what happened.

Suzy It's simple, Your Majesty. We share a flat – not that I like her but it saves the rent. Anyway, we both had babies, and hers died.

Debs No he didn't, you –

Suzy Yes he did – and you swapped him for mine.

Solomon OK, Debs, what's your side of the story?

Debs It's her baby that died – and now she wants to steal mine from me, the rotten little –

Solomon Don't start that again. Look, I'll be honest – I've got to be really sure whose baby this is, but the trouble is, I don't know you and I don't know which one to believe. If only there were some way of finding out . . .'

Narrator Solomon might have found it easier to think if the two women hadn't started arguing again.

Debs I tell you it's my child!

Suzy Rubbish! He's mine. Yours died, and you swapped them over. That's the truth of it.

Narrator Suddenly, King Solomon had a brilliant idea. He took the baby from Debs, and put it on the table. Then he turned to his servant.

Solomon Go and fetch me a sword.

Narrator Everyone wondered what Solomon was going to do. Eventually the servant came back with a big, sharp sword, and Solomon turned to Debs and Suzy.

Solomon Now, is one of you two going to tell me whose baby this really is?

Suzy I tell you it's mine. She swapped them. I'm sorry hers is dead, but she's not having mine!

Debs You little liar! You're just jealous of me – you always have been – and now you want my baby. Well you can't have him!

Solomon I don't see anything else for it. If we can't find out whose baby this is we'd better cut it in half and I'll give half to each of you.

Narrator There was a big gasp from the crowd, and then everything went quiet. Surely, he couldn't mean it? What would that achieve? Two dead babies instead of one, and two unhappy mothers? Surely, King Solomon couldn't mean to do it? The servant looked equally horrified.

Servant You must be joking!

Solomon I never joke about a thing like this. Just do what I say or it'll be worse for you.

Narrator The servant trembled as he lifted the great sword high into the air. Solomon raised his hand. When he dropped it, the servant would bring the sword down. Debs was the first to speak.

Debs Sounds fair to me – half each – and I won't have to watch her drooling over him.

Suzy No, no, no! Give him to her – give him to her – I don't want him to die! Just do anything but that. Let her have him!

Solomon Put the sword away. [*To Suzy*] Take your baby home. I can see he's yours because you loved him enough to let him go.

Narrator Suzy took her baby, crying with joy, and Solomon and his servant walked back into the palace.

Solomon You didn't think I'd really cut that child in half, did you? I just had to find out which one really loved that child, and which one just wanted him.

Narrator See? I told you Solomon was wise!

Do not abandon wisdom. (Proverbs 4:6)

Fit the following words on to the grid below:
LOVE, SWORD, JUDGEMENT, SERVANT, SOLOMON, INFANT, OWNERSHIP.

Follow the lines to see where they lead.

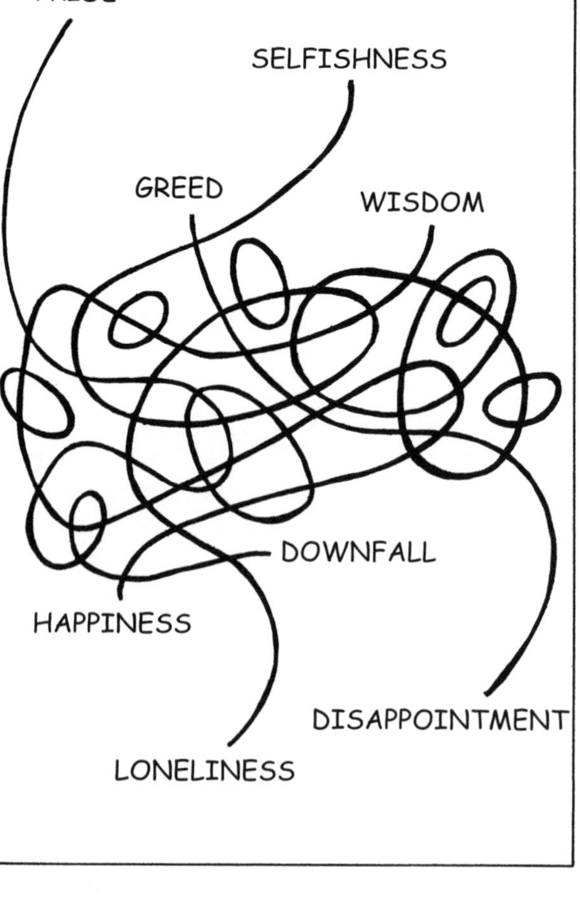

Week 3: Solomon builds the temple

Thinking about it

What's the point?

Solomon was wise, and the greatest sign of his wisdom comes in his prayer at the dedication of the temple – God's too great to be contained in our structures. Yet even now, in the twenty-first century, a lot of religious people think they've got God boxed up!

Doing it

Prayer

Thank you, God, for being so great.
We can't imagine what you're like,
and we can't measure how big you are.
And yet you care about us – thank you for that.
Help us to celebrate your love in all we do together today.
Amen.

From the known to the unknown

Have a selection of everyday items for the children to look at: tea, coffee, chocolate, a transistor radio made in Taiwan or somewhere, a bottle of French perfume, German wine – whatever. Let the children see that we are all interdependent. Without the skills and produce of other nations, we wouldn't be able to live the way we do. It reminds us of just how great creation is – and that the God who created it must be even greater.

Tell the story: 2 Chronicles 2:1-6:21

(See page 58 for a dramatised version of this story.)

Let's Build a Temple

King Solomon had a great idea, and he called his secretary. 'I want you to write a letter to King Hiram of Tyre,' he said.

'Oh, yes,' said the secretary, 'good old King Hiram. I know him well – very good friend of your father's. You know, I remember when . . .'

Solomon interrupted. 'I'm sure you do, but just take the letter, will you. It begins "Dear King Hiram. I've decided to build a temple for God . . . "'

'Ooh, that's nice,' said the secretary. 'So will God be living there permanently, so he's always right where we want him?'

Solomon sighed. 'You silly secretary-man,' he said. 'Our God's so great even heaven can't contain him, so how could we hold him in a house we built? The best this will ever be will be somewhere for us to worship. But because God's so great, we can't even build that on our own – that's why I need King Hiram's help. Ask him to send us a really good craftsman to do all the wood and metal work and all the curtains and furnishing – we need the very best he's got. Oh, and his woodcutters are far more skilled than ours, so ask him for a supply of timber.'

'That's an awful lot for him to do, Your Majesty,' said the secretary. 'D'you think we should send him some labourers to help?'

Solomon looked surprised. 'You know, that's a really good idea!' he said. 'Tell him that we'll send some workers to work alongside his people. And we'll send him enough food for all of his workers and ours, as well. OK, get that written up neatly – no smudges, now – and send it to King Hiram.'

King Hiram was really pleased. 'King David and I were such good friends,' he said, 'and now Solomon wants my help. Well, it's better than fighting each other all the time, isn't it?' So he sent a letter back to Solomon. 'I think it's great you're king,' he wrote. 'God must really care about his people to give them a wise ruler like you. Of course, I'll be glad to help. I've got a chap here called Huram. He'll work with anything – bronze, silver, gold, stone, wood – and he's handy with a needle and thread, too. Basically, if he can't work with it, you don't want it in your temple anyway.'

So Huram was sent to work with Solomon's workers and produce all the things they needed for the temple, and King Hiram got his foresters to work cutting the wood that Solomon would need. And in return, Solomon provided all the food and drink the workers could possibly want.

The temple was amazing – gold everywhere – whole walls covered in it! Even the nails they used were made of gold! Then there was cedarwood panelling, beautiful curtains – it must have been a breathtaking sight. Part of it was set aside to be the most holy part of all. It had two enormous statues with wings stretched out as if to guard the place. The wings stretched right across the room, and the statues were covered in gold. Then Solomon called his secretary again. 'We're going to bring the covenant box and put it in the holy of holies.'

'Oh, good!' exclaimed the secretary. 'Then God will be in his house.'

'I've told you before,' Solomon said sternly, 'God's too great for this house – it'll be a place to worship him. And the covenant box contains the stones with his law written on them – the ones he gave to Moses in the desert – so we've got to give that a really special place.'

So they had a big service, with lots of priests and other ministers, and put the special box in the holiest part of the temple. And Solomon said a special prayer.

'Lord God,' he said, 'you're so great even heaven itself isn't big enough for you. So I know this temple can't hold you. But let it be a sign that we love you, and want to be your people, and let it always remind us of your love and your faithfulness to us. Thank you for being such a great and wonderful God. Amen.'

A little bit later, Solomon overheard his secretary talking to the cook and telling him all about the temple. 'Now, whenever you want God,' he said, 'you'll know where to find him.'

Solomon sighed. After all he'd said about how great God is! Some people will just never learn!

Respond to the story

Discussion

Why did Solomon ask for help from the king of another country?

- Because he didn't want him to be left out?
- Because he was too lazy to do the jobs himself?
- Because he needed the particular skills that he could find there?

How did King Hiram feel?

- Put upon?
- Glad to be included?
- Pleased that his people's skills were being recognised?

Song

One or more of the following songs might be used here and/or in the all-age worship:

Each of us is a living stone
God's love is deeper
Let us sing your glory, Lord
Our God is so great
Praise God in his holy place
Surely our God is the God of gods
Take me past the outer courts

Art and craft

✔ In the centre of a large sheet of paper, do a small picture of your own church surrounded by empty space. (See 'Word and action' in the all-age worship for how this would be used.) Over the top, write Solomon's prayer: 'Even the heavens can't contain God'. Have some coloured cards – the more different colours the better – a little smaller than postcards, for the congregation to write on.

Solomon's temple.

This is the key picture, but you might want to do others in addition to it, such as:

- People felling trees
- Huram at work on a statue
- People making curtains and drapes
- Stonemasons building the walls

Drama

See the next page for a dramatised version of the story.

Drama: Let's Build a Temple

Narrator King Solomon had a great idea, and he called his secretary.

Solomon I want you to write a letter to King Hiram of Tyre.

Secretary Oh, yes, good old King Hiram. I know him well – very good friend of your father's. You know, I remember when . . .

Solomon I'm sure you do, but just take the letter, will you. It begins 'Dear King Hiram. I've decided to build a temple for God . . . '

Secretary Ooh, that's nice. So will God be living there permanently, so he's always right where we want him?

Solomon [*Sighs*] You silly secretary-man! God's so great even heaven can't contain him, so how could we hold him in a house we built? The best this will ever be will be somewhere for us to worship. But because God's so great, we can't even build that on our own – that's why I need King Hiram's help. Ask him to send us a really good craftsman to do all the wood and metal work and all the curtains and furnishing – we need the very best he's got. Oh, and his woodcutters are far more skilled than ours, so ask him for a supply of timber.

Secretary That's an awful lot for him to do, Your Majesty. D'you think we should send him some labourers to help?

Solomon [*Surprised*] You know, that's a really good idea! Tell him that we'll send some workers to work alongside his people. And we'll send him enough food for all of his workers and ours, as well. OK, get that written up neatly – no smudges, now – and send it to King Hiram.

Narrator King Hiram was really pleased.

Hiram King David and I were such good friends, and now Solomon wants my help. Well, it's better than fighting each other all the time, isn't it. Dan, take a letter. To King Solomon, Jerusalem: I think it's great you're king. God must really care about his people to give them a wise ruler like you. Of course, I'll be glad to help. I've got a chap here called Huram. He'll work with anything – bronze, silver, gold, stone, wood – and he's handy with a needle and thread, too. Basically, if he can't work with it, you don't want it in your temple anyway.

Narrator So Huram was sent to work with Solomon's workers and produce all the things they needed for the temple, and King Hiram got his foresters to work cutting the wood that Solomon would need. And in return, Solomon provided all the food and drink the workers could possibly want. The temple was amazing – gold everywhere – whole walls covered in it! Even the nails they used were made of gold! Then there was cedarwood panelling, beautiful curtains – it must have been a breathtaking sight. Part of it was set aside to be the most holy part of all. It had two enormous statues with wings stretched out as if to guard the place. The wings stretched right across the room, and the statues were covered in gold. Then Solomon called his secretary again.

Solomon We're going to bring the covenant box and put it in the holy of holies.

Secretary Oh, good! Then God will be in his house.

Solomon [*Sternly*] I've told you before, God's too great for this house – it'll be a place to worship him. And the covenant box contains the stones with his law written on them – the ones he gave to Moses in the desert – so we've got to give that a really special place.

Narrator So they had a big service, with lots of priests and other ministers, and put the special box in the holiest part of the temple. And Solomon said a special prayer.

Solomon Lord God, you're so great even heaven itself isn't big enough for you. So I know this temple can't hold you. But let it be a sign that we love you, and want to be your people, and let it always remind us of your love and your faithfulness to us. Thank you for being such a great and wonderful God. Amen.

Narrator A little bit later, Solomon overheard his secretary talking to the cook and telling him all about the temple.

Secretary Now, whenever you want God, you'll know where to find him.

Narrator Solomon sighed. After all he'd said about how great God is! Some people will just never learn!

Huram has lost his tools – can you find them? He should have a hammer, a chisel, a saw, a needle, a reel of thread and five nails.

The heaven of heavens cannot contain God. (2 Chronicles 2:6)

WORDSEARCH

Find the following words in the grid:

GOLD, CEDARWOOD, SOLOMON, HIRAM, HURAM, TEMPLE, COVENANT BOX, PRIESTS, STATUES, CURTAINS, HOLY, WORSHIP, PRAYER.

T	E	M	D	O	O	W	R	A	D	E	C
G	O	L	X	H	I	R	A	H	U	R	O
S	O	L	O	M	O	N	C	U	R	T	V
T	C	L	S	A	O	L	O	M	O	N	E
A	O	S	D	R	H	O	Y	T	W	C	N
T	V	T	A	I	T	E	M	E	O	E	A
U	E	S	T	H	U	R	A	M	R	D	N
E	N	E	U	P	R	A	D	P	S	A	T
S	A	I	E	G	O	L	F	L	H	R	B
C	U	R	T	A	I	N	S	E	I	W	O
E	G	P	R	A	Y	E	R	G	O	O	X
B	D	R	W	O	R	S	H	I	P	O	S

These two pictures may look the same but can you find 10 differences?

Week 4: All-age worship

Opening song

A song praising and celebrating the faithfulness of God

Welcome and statement of the theme

Get one or more of the children to point out or hold up the pictures as you sum up the story (breaking off from this suggested summary as necessary, in order to include the particular pictures, etc., the children have produced).

In Junior Church during the past few weeks, we've been learning about King Solomon, who was not only very wealthy but wise. First, we learnt about how Solomon became king and when God asked what gift he would like, Solomon chose wisdom. Then we saw that wisdom at work in two other stories. When two women came to Solomon quarrelling over who was the mother of a baby, Solomon used his wise understanding of people to find out the truth. And then we also learnt about Solomon's building of the temple – and his wisdom showed in that, too – in the way he went about building it, and in the prayer he offered when the temple was opened.

That's the general picture, but today we're going to concentrate on: [*Name the episode of your choice*]

Prayer

– use whichever is appropriate

Based on Week 1

Loving God,
we thank you for all the things you give us –
and especially today we thank you for the gift of wisdom.
Forgive us for the times we get our priorities wrong,
and try to find happiness in things
that cost more but are worth less,
and help us to put all our trust in you.
Through Jesus Christ our Lord, Amen.

Based on Week 2

Loving God,
we thank you for putting us among people
who love us and care about us.
We thank you also for showing us,
in your word, what love is really like.
Forgive us when we talk easily about love
but cheapen it by our actions,
and help us to reflect your true love
to the people around us. Amen.

Based on Week 3

Loving God,
thank you for being the great God you are.
Thank you for being so great
that our minds can't grasp you
and our buildings can't contain you.
Forgive us for the times when we make you seem small,
and help us to be more open to you.
Amen.

Word and action

– use whichever is appropriate

From Week 1

Play a game of *The Price is Right*. Keep the box of Common Sense discreetly out of sight to begin with as you produce the other models the children have made. You could divide the congregation into teams, trying to ensure a good age balance in each, or just let people call out their bids for the different luxury goods. As the prices are found, stick the price tag on the item and move on to the next.

Then produce your box of Common Sense and ask for a price for that. After some discussion, stick the 'Absolutely Priceless' label on it, and point out that value and price are not the same thing!

Now read the story, either in narrative or dramatised form.

From Week 2

Ask for a volunteer to pretend to be 'in prison'. If you're just using a window, let them hold the bars and peer through as though longing for freedom.

Now, you really care about this person, and want [him] to be happy. So what kinds of things could you put into the cell to achieve that? Food can be brought in every day, as can clean clothes – but what about a few creature comforts? Multi-channel TV would be good, and, of course, a computer with full internet capability.

If they haven't already asked, raise the issue yourself – why's the volunteer in prison? Explain that you're keeping the volunteer locked up because you love [him] and want [him] with you all the time. Hopefully, there will soon be a clamour for the prisoner's release! Don't give in too easily. It's a hostile world out there. What if something happens to [him]? What if [he] decides [he] doesn't want to be with you all the time? How will you cope, then?

You're now going to read a story about someone who was wise enough to know that love isn't the same as ownership.

From Week 3

Have the story read, either in narrative or dramatised form. Remind the congregation of Solomon's words: 'Even the heavens can't contain God, much less this house.' So we want to know where God's glory is seen *beyond the Church* today. Divide the congregation into groups and ask them to discuss this, and write their ideas on the multi-coloured cards. For example, maybe in your locality there are some charities or community groups that show God's love. In the wider world, events must be taking place that show God's power at work. Are there signs of hope between warring nations? Have any news stories caught people's attention? And don't forget the natural world. If people see signs of God's glory in a wonderful sunset or a pretty lily, then that's fine, too. After a short time, call them to order and ask for one or two representatives of each group to come and tell you what they've written (it doesn't matter if two groups actually agree!) and pin or stick the cards around the picture of the church. Soon you should have a really bright and attractive display. Doesn't the whole world look better when we seek God outside our own structures!

Song 2

Offering

This may be introduced with a reminder that all we give to God is really but a small recognition of the infinitely greater gifts he has given to us.

Offertory prayer

Loving God,
we thank you for all your gifts to us.
Accept what we offer here,
and help us to use all you give us wisely,
for the good of your whole creation. Amen.

Song 3

Reading

Luke 12:22-28 read from a standard Bible. Introduce it with words such as: Jesus recognised Solomon as a great king, and told us to look also for simpler and more immediate signs of God's greatness.

Talk (optional)

If you feel it appropriate (and if time permits) point out that the sheer variety of ways God's glory is shown in the world reflects just how much greater he is than we usually recognise.

Notices and family news

Prayers of intercession

These could be led entirely by the minister or other adult(s), and/or could include some prayers written by the children themselves – or simply some points that they have raised in discussion.

Song 4

Closing prayer/benediction

Unit 3
Jesus – simple greatness, gentle power

Overview of the unit

We take three key stories. They are all generally regarded as 'seasonal' stories. However, it's important that the children encounter these foundational events more than just the once each year. It's also an opportunity to deal with them in a little more depth as we see them not as isolated 'stories' but as key events characterising an entire life and gospel.

Week 1: A king of humble birth

We contrast the kingship of Jesus with that of King Herod and see the starkly different concept of greatness and power that Jesus came to offer.

Week 2: A king on a borrowed donkey

Not only a humble donkey, but he even had to borrow that! Jesus' entry into Jerusalem made a dramatic statement.

Week 3: The triumphant King of love

Talking about love is easy. Basing one's entire life on it is another matter. There are at least two distinct but related 'triumphs' here: the triumph of love over hatred and fear, which was actually won on the cross, and the triumph over death itself celebrated in the resurrection.

All-age worship

Here, you may choose to focus on any one of the three subthemes, but place it in the context of the overall story and theme: Jesus' kingship. So while the specific theme chosen will be emphasised in the choice of 'Word and action' material, some of the art and craft work the children have done in the other weeks will be used to decorate the church and set the context of the wider story.

Important note

✔ The ticked activities in Weeks 1-3 are intended as the link material for the 'Word and action' slot in the all-age worship. You will only need to do this in one of the three weeks – depending on which week's subtheme is going to be the main emphasis in the service.

Week 1: A king of humble birth

Thinking about it

What's the point?

God doesn't want to exercise coercive power, but rather the *persuasive* power of a good relationship: the power of love which can transform us, guide us and save us while leaving us free to be truly human. So he came as a baby, because only in that form could he truly appeal for our hearts' and minds' allegiance in a completely unthreatening way.

Doing it

Prayer

Lord Jesus,
thank you for loving us and wanting to share our lives.
Please share in all we do together today,
so that we can grow to know and love you
and one another more.
Amen.

From the known to the unknown

Have any of the children got a baby/younger sister/brother? Can they remember the difference their arrival made? You can talk about how a baby inspires love, partly by its very helplessness, but how it also changes the lives of everyone involved! That's rather how Jesus' birth was, as well.

Tell the story: Matthew 2:1-21

(See page 70 for a dramatised version of this story.)

The King of Fear and the King of Love

Wicked King Herod was a very frightened man. 'Someone's after my throne,' he said to Ezra, his chief bodyguard. 'I just know it – someone wants to be king in my place. Well he's not going to get it – whoever he is, he's not going to get my throne.'

Ezra tried to calm him down. 'There, there, Your Majesty,' he soothed, 'no one's out to get you – and even if they are, they'll have to get past me first.'

Just then, a servant came in. 'Sire,' he said, 'three wise men from the east have come to ask your advice.'

King Herod was flattered. 'Show them in,' he said quickly. 'And bring some food and wine – we've got to make a good impression.'

The three wise men were obviously intelligent, well-educated people – and *they* were asking *Herod's* advice! 'So, gentlemen,' he said, 'how can I help you?'

One of the men, Caspar, said, 'We wondered whether you could tell us where the new king is?'

Herod nearly fell off his throne. 'N-n-new k-k-king?' he asked. Then, remembering he had to make a good impression, he pulled himself together. 'I think you are mistaken, gentlemen. I'm the only king here.'

'Oh, no, Your Majesty,' said Melchior – another of the wise men. 'We mean a king who's only just been born. But he's definitely around here somewhere – we've seen his star in the sky and followed it here.'

Suddenly, Herod felt very cold, very sweaty and very weak. 'You're, er, quite sure about this?' he squeaked in a very un-majestic voice.

'Quite sure, Your Majesty,' all the men assured him.

Ezra thought he'd better do something before Herod lost it altogether, so he whispered, 'Your Majesty surely can't be worried about a *baby*? If you can find out where it is, we'll deal with it.'

Herod gave a big sigh of relief. Of course! 'Send for the court prophet,' he shouted. 'Now!'

'Oh, yes, sire,' said the court prophet. 'There's a prophecy in the Bible – something about the town of Bethlehem. "Don't worry about being small," it says, "because you're the town where God's great new king is going to be born." That's good,' the prophet added, 'because it's where King David came from.'

Herod was deathly pale now. 'Good?' he shrieked. 'Good? What's good about a new king? I don't want a new king – what's wrong with the old one, eh? Well? What's wrong with the old one?'

No one answered. They could have – but they didn't. Then Herod had an idea. He turned back to the three wise men. 'Well, now,' he beamed. 'Just joking, of course – just joking. Seriously, I'd like to worship this king, as well. So why don't you go to Bethlehem, find out exactly where he is, and then tell me, so that I can take him a little present? Out of the courtyard, left at the market place and just keep going, and you'll come to Bethlehem. Don't forget, now, will you? Let me know where the dear child is.'

The three wise men went to Bethlehem, and there they found the baby Jesus with his mother Mary and her husband Joseph, and they gave him presents of gold, frankincense and myrrh. What was Herod so worried about? Who could possibly be afraid of a little baby?

'I say,' said Caspar, 'he's rather lovely, isn't he?'

'Ace!' Balthazar always used fewer words than Caspar.

'He's wonderful!' said Mary. 'Isn't it amazing how one little baby can fill the whole world with love!'

That night, Caspar had a dream. An angel appeared and said, 'Don't tell Herod where you found Jesus – he's up to no good.' So the wise men went home by a different route to avoid seeing Herod again.

Herod didn't take long to realise he'd been tricked. '*They're* against me, too!' he thought. He got desperate, and hatched a horrible plan to get rid of Jesus, but God was one step ahead of him there, too. The angel went to Joseph in a dream. 'Get packing,' he said. 'You've all got to go to Egypt – Herod's getting frightened, and you know what that means.'

Joseph woke Mary, and by the time Herod's soldiers arrived in Bethlehem, Jesus was safely away in Egypt where they couldn't get to him.

Now, I ask you: what sort of a king is it that sends an army to defend him against a baby? That's probably why Herod's almost been forgotten now – but millions of people still love Jesus.

Respond to the story

Discussion

Why did Herod react the way he did?

- Just because he didn't like little boys?
- Because he was afraid of losing his throne?

Why was he afraid?

- Because he knew that everyone hated him?
- Because deep down he knew he wasn't as important as he liked to think?

Song

One or more of the following songs might be used here and/or in the all-worship:

King of kings and Lord of lords
There was one, there were two (The children's band)
Who's the King of the jungle?
You are the King of glory

Art and craft

✔ Draw or paint pictures of King Herod and the baby Jesus to put on display. (See 'Word and action' in the all-age worship for how this would be used.) Prepare some cards with words such as Power, Force, Weapons, Army, Fear, to describe Herod's resources, and others such as Love, Weakness, Needs, to apply to Jesus.

Draw or paint a picture of Jesus in Mary's arms.

This is the key picture, but you might want to do others in addition to it, such as:

- King Herod talking to the three wise men
- The three wise men following the star
- The three wise men worshipping the baby Jesus

Drama

See the next page for a dramatised version of the story.

Drama: The King of Fear and the King of Love

Narrator King Herod was very frightened. He sent for Ezra, his bodyguard.

Herod [*Ranting*] Someone's after my throne. I just know it – someone wants to be king in my place.

Ezra [*Soothingly*] There, there, Your Majesty, no one's out to get you – and even if they are, they'll have to get past me first.

Narrator Just then, a servant came in.

Servant Sire, three wise men from the east have come to ask your advice.

Herod [*Flattered*] Show them in. And bring some food and wine – we've got to make a good impression.

Narrator The three wise men were obviously intelligent, well-educated people – and *they* were asking *Herod's* advice!

Herod [*Grandly*] So, gentlemen, how can I help you?

Caspar We wondered whether you could tell us where the new king is?

Narrator Herod nearly fell off his throne.

Herod N-n-new k-k-king?

Narrator Then, remembering he had to make a good impression, he pulled himself together.

Herod I think you are mistaken, gentlemen. I'm the only king here.

Melchior Oh, no, Your Majesty – a king who's only just been born. He's definitely here somewhere – we've seen his star in the sky.

Narrator Suddenly, Herod felt very cold, very sweaty and very weak.

Herod You're, er, quite sure about this?

Wise men [*Together*] Quite sure, Your Majesty.

Narrator Ezra thought he'd better do something before Herod lost it altogether, so he whispered in his ear.

Ezra Your Majesty surely can't be worried about a baby? If you can find out where it is, we'll deal with it.

Herod [*Relieved*] Of course! Send for the court prophet. Now!

Narrator The court prophet came quickly.

Prophet Oh, yes, sire. There's a prophecy in the Bible – something about the town of Bethlehem. 'Don't worry about being small,' it says, 'because you're the town where God's great new king is going to be born.' That's good, because it's where King David came from.

Herod Good? Good? What's good about a new king? What's wrong with the old one, eh? Well? What's wrong with the old one?

Narrator No one answered. They could have – but they didn't. Then Herod had an idea. He turned back to the three wise men.

Herod Just joking, of course. Seriously, I'd like to worship this king. So go to Bethlehem, find out where he is, and then tell me, so that I can take him a little present.

Narrator The three wise men went to Bethlehem, and there they found the baby Jesus with his mother Mary and her husband Joseph, and they gave Jesus presents of gold, frankincense and myrrh.

Caspar I say, he's rather lovely, isn't he?

Balthazar Ace!

Mary He's wonderful! Isn't it amazing how one little baby can fill the whole world with love!

Narrator That night, an angel appeared to Caspar in a dream.

Angel Don't tell Herod where you found Jesus – he's up to no good. Go home by a different route to avoid seeing Herod again.

Narrator Herod didn't take long to realise he'd been tricked. He got desperate, and hatched a horrible plan to get rid of Jesus, but God was one step ahead of him there, too. The angel went to Joseph in a dream.

Angel Get packing, you've all got to go to Egypt – Herod's getting frightened, and you know what that means.

Narrator Joseph woke Mary, and by the time Herod's soldiers arrived in Bethlehem, Jesus was safely away in Egypt where they couldn't get to him. Now, I ask you: what sort of a king is it that sends an army to fight against a baby? That's probably why Herod's almost been forgotten now – but millions of people still love Jesus.

Herod is surrounded by traitors.
Can you find six of them hidden in this room?

He will reign . . . for ever. (Luke 1:33)

Help the wise men get back home without passing Herod's palace.

WORDSEARCH

Find the following words in the grid:
BETHLEHEM, HEROD, FRANKINCENSE, EGYPT, JESUS, PROPHECY, WISE, LOVE, POWER, ANGEL, GOLD, MYRRH, JOSEPH, MARY.

B	E	T	H	L	E	H	E	T	I	S	B
E	G	Y	P	L	O	N	E	W	I	S	E
J	O	S	E	P	H	P	O	W	E	S	T
Y	E	G	G	T	Y	C	E	P	O	R	H
R	N	S	Y	G	P	O	W	D	R	D	L
A	H	F	U	X	O	Y	G	O	L	D	E
M	R	R	B	S	I	L	G	R	I	S	H
F	R	A	N	K	I	N	C	E	N	S	E
G	Y	N	O	V	E	L	O	H	E	F	M
Y	M	K	R	E	W	O	P	E	G	N	A
P	R	I	O	W	E	V	H	E	W	O	D
T	I	N	N	Y	C	E	H	P	O	R	P

Week 2: A king on a borrowed donkey

Thinking about it

What's the point?

Jesus' entry into Jerusalem was seen as a challenge to the authorities. Perhaps, though, we could also see it as a challenge to the people's idea of what a king should be.

Doing it

Prayer

Lord Jesus,
thank you for being so special to us.
Please be with us in the things we do today,
and help us to learn to love you more. Amen.

From the known to the unknown

Have the children got bikes? What kinds? What kind of bike do they think the Queen rides? They will almost certainly have seen the Queen on television getting out of very expensive cars and the idea of her riding a bike may seem quite ludicrous to them. Yet, that's the equivalent of Jesus riding a donkey into Jerusalem!

Tell the story: Luke 19:28-40

(See page 76 for a dramatised version of this story.)

He's King in a Different Way

Jesus was on his way to Jerusalem – and his friends were getting excited.

'This is it,' said John to his brother James. 'He's going to take over – show them he's in charge.'

'Well, about time too,' said James. 'We've been waiting long enough – it's about time for that King Herod to find out who the real king is around here.'

'King of people's hearts is what I want to be,' Jesus reminded them, 'not the kind that bosses everyone about.' But they were so excited about the 'king' bit they never heard any of the rest.

'If you really want to do something important,' said Jesus, 'you can go and get me something to ride on when we get to Jerusalem.'

'A horse!' shouted John, gleefully. 'A big, white horse with its own armour and a proper saddle with one of those little things to put your spear in.'

'Well, a donkey actually,' Jesus answered. 'In fact, a young donkey that no one's ever ridden before.'

James was surprised. 'I know we're poor,' he said, 'but this is your one big chance. You've got to make an impression.'

'Oh, I'm going to make an impression, alright,' Jesus assured him, 'but if you think I'm going into Jerusalem done up like some kind of warlord, you've got me all wrong. Just go and get the colt for me. You'll find it just inside the village. If anyone asks you why you're taking it, just say that I need it.'

So off went James and John. 'I know what it is!' exclaimed James. 'He's playing it clever – going to sneak up on them and then strike when they're not ready.'

As he spoke, they arrived on the outskirts of Bethany where Jesus was well known. They found the colt and untied it – the owner stopped objecting when they told him who it was for – and they brought it to Jesus.

'Couldn't you have found something better than this!' scoffed Peter. 'I'm surprised it's not wearing a nappy!'

'It hasn't even got a saddle!' exclaimed Bart. 'Here, Jesus – you'd better sit on my coat.'

Some of the other disciples also put their coats on the donkey's back, and Jesus sat down. As they set out for Jerusalem there was a feeling of excitement among the disciples. They were sure this must be the big moment when God was going to give them the power to rule over everybody else.

As they got near Jerusalem, people came running to spread their coats on the road – that was their way of welcoming a great leader. On and on they travelled, with the noise growing louder all the time. People started shouting to one another about the great things they knew Jesus had done.

'He healed my daughter,' said one.

'He helped me not to feel guilty all the time,' said another.

'He cured me of a horrible disease,' a third chipped in.

'I know,' came the reply. 'If he hadn't I wouldn't be standing anywhere near to you!'

There were some people in the crowd, though, who weren't enjoying it one little bit.

Simon, the Pharisee, turned to his friend Nick and said, 'If this racket goes on, the Governor will think there's a revolution starting – and he'll blame us for it. We've got to find a way to shut this crowd up.'

'I agree,' Nick answered, 'but what can we do about it? No one's going to listen to us – they're all far too excited for that.'

'I just don't get it,' Simon grumbled. 'We look the part – all the right clothes and everything – and we're supposed to be the respected leaders around here – and no one listens to us. But give them a scruffy carpenter who hasn't combed his hair, and they're all over him.'

'Well, you must admit, he's a nice guy,' Nick pointed out, 'and he really does love people.'

'I'm getting worried about you,' Simon said, threateningly. 'You wouldn't be falling for his patter as well, would you? Anyway, love's got nothing to do with it. Religion's about good behaviour – not love.' With that, Simon pushed through the crowd to get to Jesus. 'Here,' he shouted. 'Are you going to shut these people up before some trouble starts?'

Jesus smiled at Simon. 'Shut them up?' he said. 'There's so much happiness around today that if they didn't shout the stones probably would!'

Later, as James and John returned the donkey to its owner, they were puzzled. 'What was all that about?' James wondered aloud. 'All that fuss, and he didn't make himself king. Nothing's changed.'

'Oh, I don't know,' John replied. 'I know he's not got a throne or a crown or anything, but perhaps he's our king in a different way.'

Respond to the story

Discussion

What kind of king did Jesus want to be?

- The kind that bosses people about?
- The kind that really loves people?
- One who is protected and kept separate?
- One the people can get close to?

Song

One or more of the following songs might be used here and/or in the all-age worship:

I will wave my hands
Jesus rode a donkey into town
Sing hosanna
There was one, there were two (The children's band)
We have a king who rides a donkey

Art and craft

✔ Get the children to make a display of different types of transport. (See 'Word and action' in the all-age worship for how this would be used.) You could come to the session prepared with pictures for them to paste onto a large sheet of card or paper, or you could bring a selection of magazines, newspapers, catalogues, etc., and ask them to find and cut out the pictures themselves. Either way, try and get a varied selection: helicopter, limousine, family hatchback, bicycle, milk float, delivery van – and include an obviously royal coach of some kind. Then get the children to think of the kinds of people who would use these different forms of transport, and write them on cards: rock singer, king/queen, company director, newspaper deliverer, etc. Ensure that the children understand the connection between this and the story. Jesus, being a king, might have been expected to choose something a little more majestic than a common donkey, but because his is the power of love, not force, he chose something simple – because it would show the people what kind of king he wanted to be.

Draw or paint a picture of Jesus on the donkey

This is the key picture, but you might want to do others in addition to it, such as:

- The disciples untying the donkey from the wall
- People waving branches, etc.
- Pharisees plotting together

Drama: He's King in a Different Way

Narrator Jesus was on his way to Jerusalem – and his friends James and John were getting excited.

John This is it, James. He's going to take over.

James Well, about time too. We've been waiting long enough – it's time for that King Herod to find out who the real king is around here.

Narrator Jesus was sad to hear them talking like that.

Jesus King of people's hearts is what I want to be – not the kind of king who bosses everyone about. If you really want to do something important, go and get me something to ride on.

John [*Gleefully*] A horse! A big, white horse with its own armour and a proper saddle with one of those little things to put your spear in.

Jesus Well, a donkey actually. A *young* one no one's ever ridden before.

James I know we're poor, but this is your chance to make an impression.

Jesus Oh, I'm going to make an impression, alright, but not by going into Jerusalem done up like some kind of warlord. Go and get the colt. It's just inside the village. If anyone asks, just say I need it.

Narrator So off they went. James thought he knew what Jesus was up to.

James I know what it is! He's playing it clever – going to sneak up on them and then strike when they're not ready.

Narrator As James spoke, they arrived on the outskirts of Bethany where Jesus was well known. They found the colt and untied it – the owner stopped objecting when they told him who it was for – and they brought it to Jesus. Peter wasn't impressed at all.

Peter [*Scoffing*] Couldn't you have found something better than this? Look, Bart – I'm surprised it's not wearing a nappy!

Bart It hasn't even got a saddle! Here, Jesus – sit on my coat.

Narrator Some of the other disciples also put their coats on the donkey's back, and Jesus sat down. As they set out for Jerusalem there was a feeling of excitement. The disciples were sure this must be the big moment when God was going to give them the power to rule over everybody else. As they got near Jerusalem, people came running to spread their coats on the road – that was their way of welcoming a great leader. On and on they travelled, with the noise growing louder all the time. People started shouting to one another about the great things they knew Jesus had done.

Bystander 1 He healed my daughter.

Bystander 2 He helped me not to feel guilty all the time.

Bystander 3 He cured me of a horrible disease.

Narrator There were some people in the crowd, though, who weren't enjoying it one little bit. Simon, the Pharisee, and his friend Nick.

Simon If this racket goes on, the Governor will think there's a revolution starting – and he'll blame us for it. We've got to find a way to shut this crowd up.

Nick I agree, but what can we do about it? No one's going to listen to us – they're all far too excited for that.

Simon I just don't get it. We look the part – all the right clothes and everything – and we're supposed to be the respected leaders around here – and no one listens to us. But give them a scruffy carpenter who hasn't combed his hair, and they're all over him.

Nick Well, you must admit, he's a nice guy, and he really loves people.

Simon [*Threateningly*] I'm getting worried about you. You wouldn't be falling for his patter as well, would you? Anyway, love's got nothing to do with it. Religion's about good behaviour – not love.

Narrator With that, Simon pushed through the crowd to get to Jesus.

Simon Are you going to shut these people up before trouble starts?

Jesus [*Smiling*] Shut them up? There's so much happiness around today that if they didn't shout the stones probably would!

Narrator Later, as James and John returned the donkey to its owner, they were puzzled.

James What was all that about? All that fuss, and he didn't make himself king. Nothing's changed.

John Oh, I don't know . . . I know he's not got a throne or a crown or anything, but perhaps he's our king in a different way.

Behold your King. (Zechariah 9:9)

The donkey is hiding.
Colour in the dotted shapes to find him.

G	N	I	D	I	R	J	E	S	U	J	I
P	H	A	R	I	S	Y	E	K	N	O	D
D	I	S	C	I	P	L	E	S	X	Y	R
W	O	L	A	O	C	L	B	J	U	E	S
O	R	S	E	H	L	E	N	E	P	S	E
R	O	W	W	D	T	T	V	R	H	I	E
C	S	R	O	H	B	O	J	U	A	S	S
L	O	V	A	O	L	R	E	S	R	C	I
K	I	N	G	R	P	I	R	A	I	I	R
X	Y	R	O	S	O	D	U	L	S	P	A
D	I	S	C	E	Y	U	S	E	E	L	H
H	E	A	R	T	S	N	A	M	F	E	P

WORDSEARCH
Find the following words in the grid:
PHARISEE, DONKEY, DISCIPLES, BETHANY, JESUS, JERUSALEM, CROWD, KING, LOVE, RIDING, JOY, HORSE, COLT, HEARTS.

Week 3: The triumphant King of love

Thinking about it

What's the point?

The power to hurt and destroy is really no power at all – we can all do that, and doing it doesn't make us anything special. But the power to heal, to restore, to give life – now that's real power! And it's the power of love.

Doing it

Prayer

Thank you, Lord Jesus, for giving us life
and helping us celebrate it.
Please help us to know that you're here this morning,
taking part in the things we do.
Help us to love one another in your name. Amen.

From the known to the unknown

Show the children something that's broken – perhaps a watch or an old radio that doesn't work any more. If you think it appropriate, you could also ask if any of them has ever broken something, either out of carelessness or perhaps because they were angry. We must all have done that at some time, so there's no need to be embarrassed about it, but it does show that the power to damage and destroy is nothing special – we can all do it, but hopefully we don't choose to most of the time. The power to mend, though – to heal, to give life – now that really sets someone apart. That's *real* power!

Tell the story: Passion and Resurrection narratives

(See page 82 for a dramatised version of this story.)

King of Life and Love

This is the story of how Jesus won the greatest battle in history. He didn't use guns, or swords, or anything like that, and to be honest it didn't even look, at first, as if he *had* won. But let's begin the story.

The trouble with Jesus was that he couldn't be fooled. He knew that the religious leaders weren't as perfect as they pretended to be, and when he was around other people saw it too. And that made him dangerous.

'We've got to get rid of him,' said Caiaphas, the high priest. 'He's asking too many awkward questions, and giving the people funny ideas – all that stuff about love and peace. He's a real troublemaker.'

'Got to make it look legal, though,' warned Annas, Caiaphas' father-in-law. 'We can't just bump him off – let's get the authorities to sentence him to death.'

So they got some soldiers and took Jesus to the Roman Governor, Pontius Pilate.

'He's a really dangerous man,' Caiaphas said. 'He wants to overthrow the government. He claims to be our king, and he tells people to break the law.'

Pontius Pilate saw through it straight away. 'You're just jealous of him,' he said. 'I'm going to let him go.'

Caiaphas was ready for that. 'I tell you, he's a rebel,' he said. 'And if you let him go you're no friend of the Emperor's.'

Pilate went pale. He wasn't the Emperor's favourite person as it was, and he didn't want any more trouble.

'Put him to death,' Caiaphas insisted. 'Crucify him.'

Pilate really hated Caiaphas, so he decided to make fun of him. 'You want me to crucify your *king*?'

'He's not our king,' Caiaphas retorted. 'He just says he is. The only king we've got is the Emperor.'

Pilate smiled. He'd tricked Caiaphas into saying what no good priest would ever have said. Good Jews knew that the only king they had was God – and certainly not the Roman Emperor. But then, bad people will sometimes say almost anything to get what they want.

Well, to cut a long story short, Pilate eventually gave in and had Jesus crucified. But he couldn't resist poking fun at the priests while he was doing it. He had Jesus dressed like a king in a bright purple robe, and had a crown made of horrible sharp thorns put on his head. Then he put a big notice on the cross saying, 'The King of the Jews'.

'He's not our king!' Caiaphas fumed. 'He just said he was! We'd never have a pathetic king like that!'

'Never mind,' said Annas. 'People are soon going to see Jesus for the fraud he really is. All that talk about love and peace – just wait until they drive the nails into him, and he starts cursing and swearing the way people always do. Everyone will know then that *he's* the hypocrite, not us.'

As the soldiers drove in the nails, Jesus shouted out – but it wasn't what Annas had expected. What he shouted was a prayer. 'Father God, please forgive them all – they don't know what they are doing!'

Caiaphas was horrified. 'People are going to love him even more now!' he complained. '*We* might have won the court case, but *he's* won the people's hearts.'

For once, Caiaphas was right. Jesus *had* won the people's hearts. He'd also won the most important battle – between good and evil. Whatever they did, Jesus couldn't be made to say bad things or stop loving them. In that way, he'd won. And that's one reason why the day he died came to be called '*Good* Friday'. But that wasn't the end. There was even better to come.

On the Sunday morning, some women went to visit Jesus' grave. Caiaphas had had it sealed with a big stone and guarded by soldiers because of some fantastic idea he'd got about Jesus' friends stealing his body. But as the women approached, the soldiers had gone and the grave – a big hole in the rock – was standing open with the stone rolled to one side.

While the women were wondering what to do next, a man in white clothes appeared beside them.

'Why are you looking for Jesus here?' he said. 'He's alive. No, really – alive. Go and tell his disciples that God has raised him back to life just the way he promised.'

Suddenly it all fell into place! Of course! This is what God had promised would happen – and they were the first ones to hear about it! The women ran to tell Jesus' friends, and before long everyone was talking about the Good News. Caiaphas might be high priest, and Pilate might be governor – and they might have the power to kill people they hated. But there was only one true king – the one who had the power of life and love. And now they knew that that true king was Jesus!

Respond to the story

Discussion

What were Caiaphas and Annas afraid of?

- People might listen to Jesus more than to them?
- They might lose some of their status and power?

Why did Pilate call Jesus 'king'?

- Because he wanted to mock Jesus?
- Because he thought he looked pathetic and it would embarrass Caiaphas?

Song

One or more of the following songs might be used here and/or in the all-age service:

Alleluia, alleluia, give thanks to the risen Lord
Jesus isn't dead any more
Jesus, you're the King
The Spirit lives to set us free (Walk in the light)
There was one, there were two (The children's band)

Art and craft

✔ Prepare in advance some ugly 'graffiti' (see 'Word and action' in the all-age worship for how this would be used). Use large pieces of paper (flip-chart pages would be good) and keep a second copy of each for yourself. Don't be afraid of using some common offensive symbols like swastikas – it will enhance the point about God's redemptive creativity! Get the children to work on them in groups, using whatever medium you think is appropriate – paint, crayons, felt-tips, collage, etc. – to turn your dreadful scrawls into something beautiful. You can explain that this is what God did when Jesus was crucified. He didn't destroy the cross and put something nicer in its place, but he transformed the cross, with all its pain, into a sign of life and hope. Prepare a large, ugly cross – either a picture or a model – for the congregation to transform at the service, and have ready some brightly coloured cards.

Draw or paint a picture of the empty tomb, with the cross in the background.

This is the key picture, but you might want to do others in addition to it, such as:

- Jesus on trial before Pilate
- The women coming to the tomb
- The angel at the open tomb

Drama: King of Life and Love

Leader This is the story of how Jesus won the greatest battle in history. He didn't use guns, or swords, and to be honest it didn't even look, at first, as if he *had* won. But let's begin the story.

Narrator Jesus couldn't be fooled. He knew that the religious leaders weren't perfect as they pretended, and when he was around other people saw it too. And that worried Caiaphas, the high priest and his father-in-law, Annas.

Caiaphas We've got to get rid of Jesus. He's asking too many awkward questions, and giving the people funny ideas – all that stuff about love and peace. He's a real troublemaker.

Annas Got to make it look legal, though. We can't just bump him off – let's get the authorities to sentence him to death.

Narrator So they got some soldiers and took Jesus to the Roman Governor, Pontius Pilate. Caiaphas got his word in first.

Caiaphas He's really dangerous – wants to overthrow the government. He claims to be our king, and tells people to break the law.

Narrator Pontius Pilate saw through it straight away.

Pilate You're just jealous of him. I'm going to let him go.

Caiaphas He's a rebel. If you let him go you're no friend of the Emperor's.

Narrator Pilate went pale. He wasn't the Emperor's favourite person as it was, and he didn't want any more trouble.

Caiaphas Put him to death. Crucify him. Nail him to a cross until he dies.

Narrator Pilate really hated Caiaphas, so he decided to make fun of him.

Pilate You want me to crucify your *king*?

Caiaphas He's not our king – just says he is. The only king is the Emperor.

Pilate [*Aside*] Nice one! They've never admitted *that* before!

Narrator Well, to cut a long story short, Pilate eventually gave in and had Jesus crucified. But he couldn't resist poking fun at the priests while he was doing it. He had Jesus dressed like a king in a bright purple robe, and had a crown made of horrible sharp thorns put on his head. Then he put a notice on the cross: 'King of the Jews'.

Caiaphas He's not our king! He just said he was! We'd never have a pathetic king like that!

Annas People will soon see Jesus is a fraud. All that talk about love – when they drive the nails into him, and he starts cursing the way people always do, everyone will know *he's* the hypocrite, not us.

Narrator As the soldiers drove in the nails, Jesus shouted out.

Jesus Father God, please forgive them – they don't understand!

Caiaphas [*Horrified*] People are going to love him even more, now! *We* might have won the court case, but *he's* won the people's hearts.

Narrator For once, Caiaphas was right. Jesus *had* won the most important battle – between good and evil. Whatever they did, Jesus couldn't be made to say bad things or stop loving them. In that way, he'd won. And that's one reason why the day he died is called '*Good* Friday'. But that wasn't the end. There was even better to come. On the Sunday morning, some women went to visit Jesus' grave.

Mary How are we going to get past the soldiers?

Salome Soldiers?

Mary Caiaphas had some fantastic idea about Jesus' friends stealing his body, so he put a guard on the tomb.

Other Mary Well, they're not there now.

Salome [*Mockingly*] Perhaps something frightened them off.

Other Mary Look – the tomb's open – the stone has been rolled away!

Narrator Suddenly, an angel appeared beside them.

Angel Why are you looking for Jesus here? He's alive. No, really – alive. Go and tell his disciples that God has raised him back to life just the way he promised.

Narrator Suddenly it all fell into place! Of course! This is what God had promised would happen. The women ran to tell Jesus' friends, and before long everyone was talking about the Good News. Caiaphas might be high priest, and Pilate might be governor – and they might have the power to kill people they hated. But there was only one true king – the one who had the power of life and love. And now they knew that that true king was Jesus!

Colour in the dotted shapes and complete the garden scene.

My kingship is not from this world. (John 18:36)

JESUS

Even though we can't see him, Jesus is always with us. In this space, draw a picture of him, just as a reminder.

Can you find a bit of good advice threading its way through the cross? If you want some help, look up Romans 12:21 (GNB).

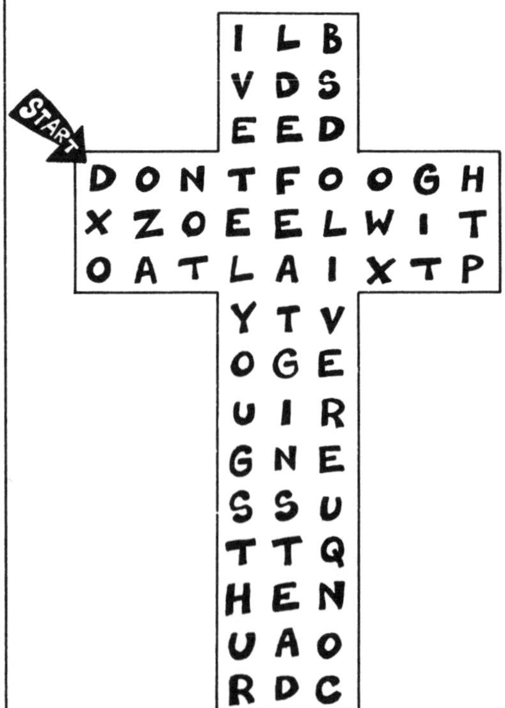

Week 4: All-age worship

Opening song

A song praising and celebrating the faithfulness of God

Welcome and statement of the theme

Get one or more of the children to point out or hold up the pictures as you sum up the story (breaking off from this suggested summary as necessary, in order to include the particular pictures, etc., the children have produced).

In Junior Church during the past few weeks, we've been learning about how Jesus is the greatest king, because his kingship is based on love not force or fear. We started off by contrasting the baby Jesus with the wicked King Herod, whose only power was to destroy, whereas Jesus was able to create love in others. Then we went on to see Jesus riding into Jerusalem on a very simple donkey, instead of the war-horse people might have expected, and lastly we saw Jesus at his crucifixion and resurrection, as the triumphant King of love – winning the battle against hatred and death with only the weapon of love.

That's the general picture, but today we're going to concentrate on: [*Name the episode of your choice*]

Prayer

– use whichever is appropriate

Based on Week 1

Loving God,
we come here to worship you.
Thank you for showing us that your power
is different from the power worldly rulers have.
Forgive us when we think and talk
as though you are like them,
and help us to show in our lives that we serve you,
and that it makes a difference.
Amen.

Based on Week 2

Loving God,
we come here to celebrate your glory,
which you show in humility.
Thank you for being a God we can get close to.
Please forgive us
for the way we sometimes make you seem remote,
and help us to show in our lives
that you are very close to us.
Amen.

Based on Week 3

Loving God,
thank you for being the giver of life and love.
We praise you because your power is the power
that creates, heals and restores.
Forgive us, please,
if we ever make you seem frightening or judgemental to others,
and help us to show your creative love in our lives. Amen.

Word and action

– use whichever is appropriate

From Week 1

Have the story read in either narrative or dramatised form. Draw attention to the display pictures of Herod and Jesus, and show the congregation the cards in random order. Ask to which character each card applies, and pin or Blue-tack the cards around the figures. Then ask whether it's as simple as that. Didn't Jesus have a kind of power that Herod couldn't understand? On the face of it, Herod was strong and the baby Jesus was weak. But if that was really the case, why did Herod feel so threatened? Perhaps the 'power' label ought to be over Jesus, and the 'weakness' label over Herod? When it came down to it, the only power Herod had was based on fear. Jesus' power was based on love. Herod had only the power to destroy, but love is the power of life!

From Week 2

Call attention to the display of different forms of transport, produce the cards and ask the congregation to decide where to put each one. The rock star might go beside a picture of a helicopter, or a very 'flash' sports car, for example. After the cards have been placed, have the story read in either narrative or dramatised form. What sort of king comes into town on a donkey's back? A very different kind of king from the kind that most of us are familiar with!

People's transport may be seen as making a statement about them – and Jesus' choice of a humble donkey made a statement about his kind of kingship.

From Week 3

Put up the copies you kept of your 'graffiti', and set the large cross at the front. Draw attention to the 'graffiti'. Not very nice, is it? Then cover each one with the children's transformed version. Emphasise to the congregation that they didn't destroy what you had done, but *used* it and *transformed* it – which is just a tiny illustration of what God did in the story that's about to be read.

Read the story, in either narrative or dramatised form, and then divide the congregation into groups. Ask them what are the 'signs of death' in your locality that need to be transformed by God's life and love into 'signs of life'. Perhaps it's environmental – waste ground that becomes a haven for nefarious goings-on. Could the council be persuaded to turn it into a sensory garden for blind people – perhaps with some help from church people? Or it may be lack of leisure facilities – could the Church help there? Ask them to write down the life-giving ideas they think of on the coloured cards. (This is a time for dreaming dreams, so don't let them worry about the details, just the vision!) After a time, call the groups to order and get one or more representatives from each group to tell the congregation their ideas and then stick or pin their cards onto the cross, transforming it from stark, deathly ugliness to a sign of life and hope for the community. The cards can be kept after the service and used by the Church's organisations and committees to focus on mission ideas, so that the 'body of Christ' may be a sign of Jesus' kingship of life and love.

Song 2

Offering

This may be introduced as a token of our recognition of Jesus' kingship in our own lives, as we bring our offerings to him.

Offertory prayer

Lord Jesus,
we offer you ourselves and our gifts.
Help us to use them well,
that the world may come to recognise
your gentle rule of love. Amen.

Song 3

Reading

1 Corinthians 1:22-31 read from a standard Bible. Introduce it with words such as: We are reminded that God not only values what seems small or silly to us, but can use it to do great things.

Talk (optional)

If you feel it appropriate (and if time permits) simply point out that Jesus accomplished much more in his 'weakness' and 'foolishness' than any of his antagonists managed in their 'strength'. We can see the reality of this in our ordinary relationships where we have to make ourselves vulnerable, refrain from the use of power and force, in order to enable real love to grow. And the story of Jesus tells us that that's God's way – and that it works!

Notices and family news

Prayers of intercession

These could be led entirely by the minister or other adult(s), and/or could include some prayers written by the children themselves – or simply some points that they have raised in discussion.

Song 4

Closing prayer/benediction